Dialectical Behavior Therapy

The Ultimate Guide to Take Control of Borderline Personality Disorders, Anxiety and Addictions. Learn Mindfulness, Interpersonal Effectiveness and Emotion Regulation

Table of Contents

Introduction

Dialectical behavioral therapy (DBT) is a kind of cognitive-behavioral therapy. Its fundamental objectives are to show individuals how to live at the time, adapt actively to stress, control feelings, and improve relationships with others.

It was initially expected for individuals with borderline personality disorder (BPD), however, it has been adjusted for different conditions where the individual struggles with emotional regulation or shows pointless conduct, such as eating disorders and substance misuse. It is, at times, used to treat post-traumatic stress disorder (PTSD).

History

DBT was created in the late 1980s by Dr. Marsha Linehan and colleagues when they found out that cognitive-behavioral therapy (CBT) alone didn't fill in just as expected in patients with BPD. Dr. Linehan and her group included procedures and built up a treatment that would meet the remarkable needs of these patients.

DBT joins a philosophical procedure called dialectics. Dialectics depend on the idea that everything is made out of alternate extremes and that change happens when there is a "dialogue" between contradicting powers, or in increasingly literary terms—thesis, antithesis, and synthesis.

All the more explicitly, dialectics makes three essential assumptions:

- Everything is interconnected.

- Change is consistent and inescapable.

- Opposites can be incorporated to shape a closer estimate of reality.

In DBT, the patient and therapist are attempting to determine the apparent inconsistency between self-acknowledgment and change to make some improvement in the patient.

Another technique offered by Linehan and her colleagues was approval. Linehan and her group learned that with support, alongside the push for change, patients were bound to collaborate and less inclined to endure trouble at the turn. The therapist approves that the individual's activities "make sense" inside the setting of their encounters without fundamentally concurring that they are the best way to deal with tackling the issue.

How It Works

DBT has developed into a proof-based psychotherapy approach for an assortment of conditions. When an individual is experiencing DBT, they can hope to take an interest in three helpful settings:

- A group setting where an individual is shown conduct aptitudes by doing schoolwork assignments and pretending better approaches for collaborating with individuals.

- Individual therapy with a professional where those educated behavioral abilities are adjusted to the individual's very own life challenges.

- Telephone coaching in which an individual can call their therapist in the middle of meetings to get direction on adapting to a troublesome right now circumstance.

In DBT, individual therapists meet with an interview group to assist them in managing the emotional demands of rewarding their patients and exploring troublesome and complex issues.

While every therapeutic setting has its set structure and objectives, the accompanying attributes of DBT are found in group skills training, singular psychotherapy, and telephone coaching:

Support: You'll be urged to perceive your positive qualities, properties, create and use them.

Behavioral: You'll figure out how to investigate any issue or ruinous standards of conduct and supplant them with solid and powerful ones.

Cognitive: You'll focus on changing thoughts, beliefs, conduct, or activities that are not successful or supportive.

Ranges of abilities: You'll learn new skills to improve your capacities.

Acceptance and change: You'll learn strategies to acknowledge and endure your life, feelings, and yourself just as abilities to assist you in rolling out improvements in your behaviors and associations with others.

Collaboration: You'll figure out how to express and cooperate as a team (psychiatrist, group therapist, and therapist).

DBT Strategies

Individuals experiencing DBT are trained on how to change their conduct, utilizing four main strategies adequately.

Core Mindfulness

Mindfulness skills, which is maybe the most important strategy in DBT, instruct you to concentrate on the present or "live at the time." By doing this, you can figure out how to focus on what's happening within you (thoughts, emotions, sensations, impulses) just as what's outside of you (what you see, hear, smell, and touch) in non-judgmental ways. These skills will assist you in slowing down so you can concentrate on healthy coping skills amidst passionate torment. Mindfulness can help you stay quiet, abstain from participating in automatic negative idea designs, and impulsive behavior.

Focus on your breath. Observe the vibe of breathing in and breathing out, watching your paunch rise and fall as you relax.

Distress Tolerance

Distress tolerance instructs you to acknowledge yourself and the present circumstance. All the more explicitly, you figure out how to endure or survive a crisis utilizing four procedures: interruption, self-relieving, improving the occasion, and considering the advantages and disadvantages of not enduring trouble. By learning distress tolerance techniques, you'll have the option to get ready ahead of time for any severe feelings and adapt to them with a progressively positive long-term outlook.

Run all over the steps; in case you're inside, head outside. In case you're sitting, get up and stroll around. The point is to occupy yourself by permitting your feelings to follow your body.

Interpersonal Effectiveness

Interpersonal effectiveness encourages you to become progressively emphatic in a relationship (for instance, communicating needs and saying "no") while keeping that relationship positive and healthy. This occurs by figuring out how to tune in and convey adequately, manage troublesome individuals, and regard yourself as well as other people.

Emotion Regulation

Emotion regulation gives a lot of aptitudes that cause one all the more successfully to explore incredible emotions. It instructs you to your feelings. By perceiving and adapting to extraordinary negative feelings (for instance, anger), you can decrease your emotional vulnerability and have increasingly positive, passionate encounters.

Recognize how you're feeling and do the inverse. In case you're dismal and want to pull back from loved ones, do the inverse. Make plans to see loved ones and remain social.

Is DBT Right for You?

While most of the researches to date have concentrated on the adequacy of DBT for individuals with borderline personality disorder who struggles with contemplations of self-destruction and self-harm, DBT has been utilized in the treatment of an assortment of psychological well-being conditions including:

- Attention-deficit/hyperactivity disorder (ADHD)

- Binge eating disorder

- Bipolar confusion

- Bulimia

- Generalized anxiety disorder

- Major depressive disorder (counting treatment-resistant major depression and incessant sadness)

- Post-traumatic stress disorder

- Substance use disorder

Researchers have discovered that DBT is compelling to pay little heed to age, sex, sexual orientation, and race/ethnicity. The ideal approach to know if DBT is directly for you is to converse with psychological well-being proficient, who will assess your indications, treatment history, and therapy goals to decide the best next step.

If you accept that you, a friend or family member, may benefit from DBT if it's not too much trouble, look for direction from a specialist or healthcare professional prepared in this treatment approach. DBT specialists aren't, in every case, easy to find.

You can start your search with the Clinical Resource Directory kept up by Behavioral Tech, an association established by Dr. Linehan, to prepare mental health professionals in DBT. This registry permits you to look by the state for clinicians and projects that have experienced DBT making with Behavioral Tech, LLC, or the Behavioral Research and Therapy Clinics at the University of Washington. Another alternative is to ask your doctor, advisor, or another psychological wellness expert to allude you to somebody who works in DBT.

Chapter 1 - DBT vs. CBT: How do they differ?

Psychotherapy is outstanding amongst other treatment methods accessible for various psychological sicknesses. One of the most well-known kinds of treatment is called Cognitive Behavioral Therapy (CBT). Also called "talk therapy," CBT centers on discussing your issues to assist you in unexpectedly encircling your considerations. If you feel like negative thoughts are consistently in charge–"I am a failure. I can't do anything right. Nobody will like me if they see who I truly am."–CBT can assist you by utilizing the rationale and motivation to turn the tables and be in charge of your thoughts instead of permitting your thoughts to control you.

CBT cycle

CBT depends on the possibility that our thoughts and acts impact our emotions, so changing how we consider and respond to circumstances will assist us in feeling much better. In any case, standard CBT isn't successful in rewarding every single psychological instability.

Another regular sort of treatment is called Dialectical Behavior Therapy (DBT). DBT is an increasingly explicit type of CBT that centers on helping individuals who will, in general, have extreme emotional reactions and collaborate with the earth around them in a less emotional, more advantageous way

With such comparable names, are CBT and DBT not quite the same as one another? And can using one have benefits over using the other? Peruse on to find out about the contrasts between CBT and DBT, and how to know which one will best assist you.

CBT is a General Term

CBT is a catch-all phrase for treatments that share normal qualities. DBT is a type of CBT, alongside a few different types. Therapists who practice CBT by and large practice talk treatment that depends on a few controlling highlights. Those include:

Treats Emotional Response: In light of the possibility that our thoughts impact our emotions, changing how we consider and respond to circumstances will assist us in feeling much better.

Constrained to a Specific period: Most patients will look for treatment dnt for a timeframe and afterward begin to apply CBT strategies all alone without noteworthy help from a mental health professional. If the state of mind or behavioral problems persist, clients may then advance to an alternate type of therapy to address a specific trauma or another issue that keeps on causing torment or be an obstruction to healthy living.

Having a Good Therapist-Patient Relationship: CBT works best when the patient feels like they can confide in their therapist. Due to their idea of treatment, patients should search out somebody they regard and feel confident with.

Depends on Cognition and Rationale: CBT urges patients to apply logic and reason to help direct how they react to circumstances instead of letting feelings do all the driving.

Utilizations Structure to Guide Treatment: specialists have a particular explanation behind the strategies and techniques they raise in every meeting. They utilize the client's objectives to make sense of which CBT ideas will be generally valuable to them and tailor everyone in like manner.

While DBT is a kind of CBT, it is tailored towards helping individuals recognize the pain and inconvenience they feel, yet still have a sense of security and "ok" at the time and engaged in picking sound practices rather than hasty or unsafe activities. While some accentuation is put on managing thoughts, patients are educated to recognize triggers outside of themselves and match those triggers with a reliable method for dealing with stress or reaction.

CBT vs. DBT for Treating Certain Illnesses

Not every mental illness react to treatment similarly. A therapy technique that functions admirably for depression and tension can fuel eating and personality disorders.

CBT has been demonstrated to be fantastically successful while treating depression and is bound to cause depression to go into decline than different kinds of therapy. This method of therapy has been demonstrated advantageous in treating anxiety, as it gives patients power over their recuperation. CBT has additionally been appeared to help with over the obsessive-compulsive disorder (OCD), fears, panic disorder, post-traumatic stress disorder, and sleeping issues.

DBT was made to help those determined to have a borderline personality disorder. DBT centers on assisting individuals in changing their behavioral patterns, instead of attempting to think or talk through the issues they are struggling with. This kind of CBT enables the individuals who have created examples of severe emotional reactions and impulsive behaviors in light of what patients depict as overpowering emotions of pain and reaction—the sentiment of walking through a world loaded up with knives. DBT frequently is an effective therapy for individuals who struggle with self-harm practices like cutting and chronic suicidal ideation. Sexual trauma survivors additionally react well to DBT techniques.

Ways of thinking Used in CBT vs. DBT

CBT centers on thinking and rationale, as most ordinarily found in the stoic philosophy of thought and the Socratic Method. The Socratic Method utilizes critical thinking to address presumptions set up. This functions admirably for the individuals who endure with anxiety and depression, as it encourages them to see their issues from an increasingly logical perspective. For instance, clients who struggle with emotions of disappointment and insufficiency are approached to look at the realities. When have they, in actuality, been fruitful at achieving a goal? Are there others—companions, family, or colleagues—who could give evidence of the client's achievement in various circumstances? Who or what are they using as a measuring stick for progress? Is that a realistic comparison?

DBT depends intensely on care aptitudes utilized in Buddhism and Zen practices. DBT trains patients to use specific mindfulness techniques to figure out how to live with pain in the world and acknowledge how things are as opposed to enduring by attempting to transform them.

The Difference in Treatment Methods

CBT centers on how your thoughts, emotions, and behavior impact one another. While DBT accomplishes take a shot at these things, accentuation is given more towards controlling feelings, being careful, and figuring out how to acknowledge the pain. CBT tries to enable patients to perceive when their thoughts may get problematic and gives them methods to divert those contemplations. DBT causes patients to discover approaches to acknowledge themselves, have a sense of security, and deal with their feelings to help direct possibly destructive and harmful practices.

Clients who take part in DBT therapy take an interest in DBT skills training sessions that are usually educated in a group setting in four modules. Most patients additionally meet week after week with a DBT therapist or DBT mentor and get DBT phone training varying when they need assistance the most. Sometimes, when patients can utilize DBT skills to manage their feelings, practice care, and improve relationships with others, they can change to progressively standard CBT groups to address specific negative thought patterns or repeating harmful behaviors.

Instructions to tell if CBT or DBT is Right for You

The ideal approach to make sense of which kind of treatment is best for you is to talk with a mental health professional—a psychiatrist, therapist, or psychologist. They will think about your side effects, treatment history, the objectives you plot for what you ask for from therapy, and suggest the best subsequent stages.

What Is Your Diagnosis?

Since every sickness reacts diversely to treatment techniques, you will need to go with the method that has been indicated best for rewarding your diagnosis and symptoms. If you have not yet gotten a determination from a psychiatrist or psychologist, think about setting an arrangement for psychiatric diagnosis and psychological testing. This will assist you in distinguishing the best treatment options, just as qualities and existing aptitudes you can use in your recovery process.

Depression and anxiety victims have discovered a great deal of progress with CBT, while individuals with borderline personality disorder and constant considerations of self-destruction discover DBT progressively supportive. Remember that numerous individuals have more than one diagnosis, and at some point, individuals use components from both DBT and CBT to deal with their symptoms.

Have You Tried Therapy Already?

Numerous people who have gone to therapy say they would prefer not to return since they feel like it wasn't overpowering. Since the patient-therapist relationship is so significant, consider meeting a couple of different therapists to check whether you can locate a superior match. You may as well need to consider attempting an alternate "flavor" of CBT. Notwithstanding DBT, there is a whole alphabet soup of different variations of CBT, including Acceptance and Commitment Therapy (ACT) and Mindfulness-Based Cognitive Therapy (MBCT). If a goal of therapy is to improve your relationships with others, consider attempting couples treatment or family therapy instead of going alone.

Furthermore, give it half a month before you throw in the towel. Recall that your therapist won't accomplish the work for you. You should focus on achieving the difficult task of making changes throughout your life to help more advantageous reasoning, more beneficial practices, and more fruitful living. Recovery doesn't occur incidentally; however, by utilizing a treatment coordinated to your side effects and finding the right therapist or psychiatric treatment program, you can, bit by bit, make a progression of little switches that indicate less pain and superior life.

With such a significant number of treatment choices out there, it tends to be confounding to recognize what methods will best assist you. CBT and DBT are a portion of the most typical therapy practices and have been appearing to help people experiencing various mental illnesses. Skyland Trail offers both CBT and DBT in our residential treatment and day treatment programs. Contact our admissions group to get familiar with how our emotional well-being treatment projects may support you, a friend, or a family member.

They were developed for various purposes

DBT was grown explicitly to treat individuals with a borderline personality disorder, which is described by unstable feelings and interpersonal conflict. Owing to this, self-acknowledgment, approving emotional experiences, and directing feelings are altogether vigorously underscored in DBT. Traditional CBT is very change-centered. Patients figure out how to distinguish unfortunate, twisted thinking, and supplant it with more advantageous, progressively target thinking, a procedure called cognitive restructuring. The creator of DBT, Marsha Linehan, found out that her patients opposed the change-focused approach of CBT; thus, she started consolidating components like care and acknowledgment as a way of approving her patients' present emotional experiences. The "dialectical" part of DBT originates from this endeavor to find some kind of harmony between acceptance and change.

DBT is more structured

CBT is somewhat similar to a psychotherapeutic toolbox. A patient comes in with a specific issue, and the therapist can choose certain cognitive restructuring techniques or behavioral learning techniques to enable the patient to take care of the issue. They usually meet once per week, and the patient will work on utilizing the new technology between meetings. Even though CBT protocols are genuinely standard, the therapist chooses to utilize relies upon the patient's particular issues. DBT is a higher amount of a boxed set of explicit CBT methods, and everybody gets a similar essential treatment paying little mind to their condition. These incorporate mindfulness skills, interpersonal effectiveness, distress tolerance, and emotional regulation. These skills are particularly helpful for the sorts of issues DBT was created to treat, such as borderline personality disorder, impulse control problems, self-destructive thoughts, eating disorders, complex PTSD, anger management problems, and addiction. A CBT therapist will meet with you once every week and allocate homework for you to do between sessions. However, in DBT, you will meet two times every week, once separately and once with the group. You may be urged to contact your therapist during the week if you are experiencing difficulty. Since DBT is regularly used to treat individuals with drive control issues, such as emotional outbursts and addiction, it's frequently useful, or even essential, to have a lifesaver between meetings. Similarly, somebody in AA can call their support if she needs to drink.

DBT concentrates more on acceptance

Of the four principal components of DB—mindfulness abilities, relational viability, trouble resilience, and emotional regulation; two of them, interpersonal effectiveness and emotional regulation, center on change, while the other two, mindfulness and distress tolerance, center on acknowledgment. This became out of a requirement for patients to feel approved in their emotional experience. However, these patients' increased emotional activity additionally makes it more outlandish that cognitive rebuilding alone will be 100% powerful. Since emotional responses can heighten so rapidly, they need to figure out how to endure enthusiastic trouble sufficiently long to utilize techniques of emotional regulation and interpersonal effectiveness. For instance, if you suddenly feel overpowered by anger, it's difficult to stop and challenge the contemplations behind that outrage. A progressively useful strategy may be to concentrate on the physical sensations of the anger or practice deep breathing.

DBT incorporates a group element

Regularly, DBT will incorporate one individual session and one group session every week. The patient expresses explicit issues with the therapist exclusively and afterward rehearses center DBT abilities in the group sessions. DBT incorporates a group component since unstable feelings regularly lead to stormy relationships. Emotional swings don't occur in a vacuum; they rely upon setting, notably social setting. Learning interpersonal effectiveness and different abilities are increasingly viable with regards to a group, where individuals can practice new skills in a strong situation. The group sessions make DBT particularly appropriate for treating addiction. It's considerable the amount of pressure individuals face while recouping from social dependence. These may be general, similar to ordinary family clashes or relational worry at work, or they might be increasingly explicit to addiction, such as companions compelling you to utilize once more. Practicing DBT skills with the group better sets you up to confront those weights in the wake of leaving treatment. It also causes you to improve your relationships with supportive loved ones. Having a strong support network of people is one of the most significant methods of shielding yourself from relapse.

DBT takes longer

CBT centers on specific problems. Therapists meet with patients once a week, and treatment commonly keeps going on for a while. When the protocol is finished, the patient has the right tools to deal with the issue. In DBT, patients come twice a week—once for an individual session and once for a group session and treatment may last for half year or a year. There are two main reasons for this.

To start with, DBT shows a set-up of aptitudes, while CBT just concentrates on one or two. It usually takes more time to learn four center abilities than one. Regularly, patients with DBT experience the ill effects of increasingly extreme conditions—borderline personality disorder, addiction, severe eating disorders, complex PTSD, etc. These conditions are all the more profoundly established or have a natural segment that just makes them harder to treat. In any case, DBT has been demonstrated to be viable in rewarding these conditions.

Both CBT and DBT are effective

Both CBT and DBT are supported by extensive research and are successful methods of treating a wide range of conditions. Which type of therapy you use will rely upon your particular circumstance, and a skilled therapist can assist you in deciding which is probably going to work better for you.

Chapter 2 - Some of the myths surrounding DBT

Borderline personality disorder (BPD) is a widespread condition with the ability to influence each part of an individual's life, including their temperament, practices, and relationships. Fortunately, mental health disorder is increasing a more extensive comprehension among the overall population, yet numerous misguided judgments remain.

Here are 11 myths and facts about borderline personality disorder.

Myth 1: BPD is certainly not an accurate diagnosis

Fact: BPD is a generally acknowledged emotional wellness analysis.

For almost 40 years, the American Psychiatric Association (APA) has formally perceived borderline personality disorder as a real emotional well-being conclusion in their distribution, The Diagnostic and Statistical Manual of Mental Disorders (DSM). The DSM is the standard text professional use to diagnose psychological wellness conditions.

Depreciators may accept that individuals with BPD side effects are excessively emotional or attention-seekers, however, this position is mistaken and destructive. Individuals with BPD loath or advantage from the condition since it can cause chaos in their life.

Myth 2: Only women have a borderline personality disorder

Fact: Women make up the most significant part. However, anybody can have BPD.

The facts demonstrate that many people who have BPD are ladies, yet it is off base to state that lone ladies have the condition.

Things being what they are, men make up around 25%, surprisingly with BPD. The myth that solitary ladies have BPD is destructive in their mistake due to the possible stigma. A man with side effects of BPD might be increasingly hesitant to look for treatment for fear that he will be judged harshly by friends and family, treatment experts, or society. A woman may feel like she can't get an unbiased evaluation since everybody will expect she has BPD essentially as a result of her sex.

Myth 3: BPD is brought about by childhood trauma

Certainty: Childhood trauma is a risk factor, not a single reason.

The theory that childhood trauma causes BPD is mostly right. Psychological wellness conditions have risk factors that expand the chances of the disorder forming.

The National Institute on Mental Health reports that BPD risks factors include:

Family history – individuals with parents or siblings who have BPD are bound to have the condition.

Brain/biological influence – individuals with BPD, have unexplained brain changes in the areas that control driving forces and feelings.

Environment and social factors – traumatic life events like maltreatment or abandonment during adolescence appear to trigger BPD side effects.

Myth 4: Borderline Personality Disorder is rare

Fact: BPD influences millions.

As it were, all psychological wellness conditions are uncommon because they speak to atypical side effects and levels of working. Many people don't have emotional wellness conditions, and the vast majority with psychological wellness conditions don't have BPD.

In any case, BPD influences a considerable number of individuals. The specific quantities of BPD diagnoses are trying to assemble. Yet, it evaluates that between 2% and 6% of individuals in the United States will have BPD sooner or later in their lives.

This measurement implies that in any event, 1 of every 50 individuals will be determined to have BPD.

Myth 5: People with BPD are manipulative and attention-seeking

Fact: People with BPD act from numerous points of view, however, that they need to.

You may accept the myth that individuals with BPD take part in manipulation and attention-seeking behaviors since they like it. Having BPD is certifiably not a comfortable situation. The condition is interchangeable with stress, tension, and unhappiness.

If somebody with BPD is carrying on through manipulation or seeming to look for consideration, it is because of their distress to feel well and keep away from partition or rejection. S, their unfortunate adapting abilities create en route as they can't discover the help they look for. Lying and control are just a bombed endeavor to control side effects.

Myth 6: Suicide threats by people with BPD aren't severe

Fact: All suicidal threats ought to be paid attention to.

Individuals may erroneously observe suicidal threats from somebody with BPD as an approach to make a response. Once more, this supposition is false and unreasonable.

Individuals with BPD experience a high pace of suicide. Upwards of 10% of individuals with BPD will end it all while a lot more will participate in a suicide attempt and self-hurt.

All suicide attempts must be paid attention to. The risks of overlooking the threats are excessively high.

Myth 7: DBT is the primary therapy for BPD

Fact: DBT is only one effective treatment for BPD.

Dialectical behavioral therapy (DBT) is a type of talk treatment explicitly intended to treat indications related to BPD like chronic suicidality and emotional inconsistency. The researcher arranged evidence indicating that DBT is powerful in rewarding BPD.

Although DBT is a good option, others exist. For instance, cognitive-behavioral therapy (CBT) is the establishment of some parts of DBT. Additionally, mental health treatment that straightforwardly targets causes and hazard components of BPD could help decrease manifestations.

As usual, it is imperative to take note that there isn't one treatment approach that works for everybody. Medicines must be tailored to a person's exceptional needs and encounters.

Myth 8: People with BPD aren't fit for affection

Fact: Everyone is fit for affection.

Such a sweeping and skeptical perspective on individuals with BPD isn't right.

Individuals with BPD can cherish and be adored. Numerous

with BPD is in the long term, serious relationships that persevere through the equivalent high points and low points of different connections.

Individuals with BPD struggle to control their feelings and deal with their practices. Their states of mind can go from glad to bad-tempered to pitiful, rapidly. Their impulsivity may prompt lamentable activities.

These issues can make relationships all the more challenging, so tolerance from all parties is a necessity.

Myth 9: People with BPD are unbearable

Fact: People with BPD can be colossal, kind, and adoring individuals.

Unbearable is a strong word and one that doesn't make a difference to all individuals with BPD. Individuals have times where they are not pleased with their activities or how they took care of a circumstance. However, they discover absolution and push ahead.

Living with or being involved with any individual who has a psychological sickness, physical ailment, or other test is a difficult experience. However, that doesn't mean it is inconceivable. Individuals with BPD who get treatment can be more joyful than they were to discover soundness in life after treatment.

Myth 10: People with BPD are dangerous

Fact: People with BPD are bound to hurt themselves than any other individual.

It is genuine individuals with BPD can have times of peevishness. One of the main diagnostic criteria for BPD is a powerfully, improper level of anger.

Individuals with BPD may:

- Have a bad temper or a short wire

- Appear to be irate continually

- Get into physical confrontations

This displeasure doesn't mean they are a threat to other people. As referenced, individuals with BPD have a high suicide rate, so they represent the most severe threat to themselves, not others.

Myth 11: Borderline character disorder isn't treatable

Fact: Treatment assists individuals in BPD feel and capacity better.

Here is another perilously mistaken legend. If individuals accept borderline personality disorder can't be viably rewarded, they may never initiate mental health services.

BPD is an unpredictable and testing condition. There are two keys to making BPD treatment effective:

1. **Evidence-based treatments** – People may offer a wide range of solutions for BPD, yet if the treatment makes unreasonable guarantees, it may be unrealistic. Choices like DBT and CBT have been demonstrated viable. Additionally, meds like antidepressants and state of mind stabilizers are magnificent decisions when joined with treatment.

2. **Start early** – To build the odds of recuperation from BPD, treatment needs to start as quickly as time permits and proceed for an all-inclusive period. I am standing by too long to even think about beginning grants the negative coping skills to get instilled and harder to change.

Chapter 3 - What Disorders Does DBT Treat?

Dialectical behavioral therapy (DBT) is a type of cognitive-behavioral therapy. Cognitive-behavioral therapy attempts to distinguish and change negative thinking patterns and pushes for positive behavioral changes.

DBT might be utilized to treat suicidal and other pointless practices. It encourages the patient's abilities to adapt to, and change, unhealthy behaviors.

What's Unique About Dialectical Behavioral Therapy?

The expression "dialectical" originates from the possibility that uniting two alternate extremes in treatment—acknowledgment, and change—brings superior outcomes over it is possible that only one.

A one of a kind part of DBT is its emphasis on the acknowledgment of a patient's experience as a path for therapists to console them—and balance the work expected to change negative practices.

Standard comprehensive DBT has four parts:

- Individual therapy
- Group skills training
- Telephone coaching, if necessary for emergencies between sessions
- Consultation group for medicinal services providers to remain motivated and talk about patient care

Patients consent to do homework to rehearse new abilities. This incorporates rounding out day by day "diary cards" to follow more than 40 emotions, urges, practices, and aptitudes, such as lying, self-injury, or self-respect.

What Conditions Does DBT Treat?

Dialectical behavioral therapy centers around high-chance, tough-to-treat patients. These patients regularly have numerous diagnoses.

DBT was at first intended to treat individuals with suicidal behavior and borderline personality disorder. In any case, it has been adjusted for other psychological well-being issues that undermine an individual's security, relationships, work, and emotional well-being.

A borderline personality disorder is a disorder that prompts intense emotional distress. Patients may have severe anger explosions and aggression, moods that move quickly, and extreme sensitivity to rejection.

Individuals with a borderline personality disorder may experience issues directing feelings. They experience shakiness in:

- Moods

- Behavior

- Self-image

- Thinking

- Relationships

Impulsive behavior, such as substance abuse, risky sex, self-injury, and rehashed life emergencies, legal troubles, and homelessness, are normal.

The American Psychiatric Association has embraced DBT as successful in rewarding borderline personality disorder. Patients who experience DBT have seen enhancements, for example:

- Less constant and less severe suicidal behavior

- Shorter hospitalizations

- Less annoyance

- More reluctant to drop out of treatment

- Improved social working

Substance abuse is normal with a marginal character disorder. DBT assists substance abusers with a borderline personality disorder. However, it hasn't demonstrated compelling for addiction alone.

Scientists are examining whether DBT might be compelling in treating these conditions:

- Mood disorder

- Binge eating

- ADHD

- Post-traumatic stress disorder

Distress tolerance

Sooner or later, everybody faces extreme emotional states and changes. For specific individuals, the nearness of overpowering or uncontrolled feelings in light of stress happens routinely. Distress tolerance depicts a person's capacity to deal with their internal emotional state, it pressures instigating factors. If somebody has a low misery resilience, they will probably get overpowered by mildly stressful situations, conceivably reacting in negative mental and behavioral ways.

Luckily, for people who struggle with an unseemly stress response, a few remedial methodologies may demonstrate supportively. Generally, treatment regularly centered on unpleasant situational evasion, however more up to date practices and treatments have risen, which people both can seek after all alone or with the guide of care professional. These more up to date treatment modalities include grasping the unpleasant situation(s) and figuring out how to draw in with them fittingly. One popular new treatment is called dialectical behavioral therapy (DBT). It includes a combination of psychologists and psychotherapy (talk treatment), to assist patients in building sufficient distress tolerance skills for ideal living.

Significance for Patients

Visit times of severe emotional distress can be devastating on a wide range of levels. Visit or uncontrollable stress can affect the body, the disposition, and the brain. This incorporates side effects like migraine, muscle strain, weariness, sleep problems, anxiety, eagerness, over or undereating, touchiness, angry outbursts, emotions of overpowering, social withdrawal, and change in sex drive. These indications can harm social or conjugal connections, decline work execution, unleash devastation on the physical body, and overall quality of life.

Distress tolerance is a need in circumstances where a person's stress factor can't be avoided, or the individual has no reasonable methods for getting away from their negative feelings. Distress tolerance skills for anxiety and despair (all-inclusive affect more than 500 million individuals) have demonstrated critical in the present social insurance scene. Building the right pressure taking care of abilities is additionally especially significant for patients who experience the ill effects of any sort of psychological instability, as they can be life-putting something aside for those in the risk of self-harm.

Common Practices and Strategies

The basics of distress tolerance revolve around an individual getting increasingly mindful of their internal emotional state and its impact on their present idea examples or activities. A patient needs to get familiar with the act of self-relieving, or the capacity to both quiet the body and keep up mindfulness. Regular practices for self-relieving that patients can utilize at home as well as all alone incorporate controlled breathing, meditation, yoga, and progressive muscle relaxation.

According the National Alliance on Mental Illness, distress tolerance expertise work must incorporate a person's improvement of a constructive character and the capacity to steadily oversee deep down coordinated adverse feelings. Numerous individuals decide to fuse tangible objects, rewards, or physical activities into their schedules of self-relieving and actual character work. This may remember reveling for a small snack, working out, or tuning in to the main tune in light of extraordinary negative feeling. Care must be taken with these practices, as they are proper behavioral reactions when used healthily.

Embracing Radical Acceptance

Many care suppliers guarantee that the idea of basic acknowledgment is a key fixing in the improvement of distress tolerance, and they effectively urge their patients to grasp the thought completely. Radical acceptance applies to circumstances in which the wellspring of the painful or devastating feelings can't be stayed away from, so an individual should rather figure out how to accept them. Since a patient can't avoid from the source(s) of their agony, they have to figure out how to face it and (ideally) gradually change how they feel about it after some time.

This process can't and doesn't occur incidentally. Radical

acceptance regularly happens in a few phases. Four basic skills that are educated in these stages are:

- **Distraction**: The capacity to move a negative idea to an increasingly charming spot; lack of bias

- **Self-mitigating:** The capacity to "support self;" frequently through the commitment of the five detects

- **Improving the moment:** The capacity to utilize positive mental imagery to enhance a distressing circumstance

- **Concentrate on advantages and disadvantages**: The capacity to list the upsides and downsides of tolerating or not tolerating the unpleasant circumstance well; past ramifications for past poor reactions might be raised as cons

The improvement of these skills in light of unpleasant circumstances should ease patients towards a state where the two of them can acknowledge their world and control their responses to that reality.

Skill No. 1: Distracting

The primary ability, diverting, assists clients in changing their concentration from upsetting thoughts and feelings to progressively engaging or neutral activities. This ability is instructed with the abbreviation ACCEPTS:

A – Is for activities and diverting oneself with healthy, pleasant interests, such as leisure activities, exercise, and chatting with companions.

C – Is for contributing and getting things done to help other people through chipping in or only a thoughtful gesture.

C – Is for contrasting oneself with those less lucky, seeing reasons as appreciative.

E – Is for emotions, distinguishing the present negative feeling and acting oppositely, such as moving or singing when feeling pitiful.

P – Is for pushing away, by intellectually leaving the present circumstance and concentrating on something charming and detached to the current conditions.

T – Is for thoughts, occupying one's attention from the negative emotions with random and neural thoughts, such as tallying things, or doing a riddle.

S – Is for sensations, and diverting oneself with physical sensations utilizing numerous faculties, such as holding an ice 3D shape, drinking a hot refreshment, or appreciating a warm foot soak.

Skill No. 2: Self-Soothing

The subsequent skill in distress tolerance is self-alleviating; clients can utilize the five senses to sustain themselves in a variety of ways:

1. **Vision:** Look at lovely things, such as flowers, art, landscapes, or creative execution.

2. **Hearing:** Listen to music, exuberant or delicate, or appreciate the scents of nature, such as birds chirping and waves smashing. Relish the voice of a family member or companion.

3. **Smell**: Use a lotion or fragrance, light a scented flame, notice the aromas of nature, or heat a sweet-smelling formula.

4. **Taste:** Enjoy a healthy supper or enjoy wonton pastry—a trial with another flavor or texture, and spotlight on the food's flavors.

5. **Touch:** Pet an animal or give somebody an embrace. Have a back rub, rub on lotion, or cuddle up in a delicate cover.

Skill No. 3: Improving the Moment

In the third distress tolerance skill, the goal is to utilize positive mental symbolism to improve one's present circumstance. The abbreviation for this expertise is "IMPROVE":

I – Is for imagery, such as imagining a loosening up scene or a successful interaction. Envision negative emotions melting away.

M – Is for making importance or reason from a troublesome circumstance or pain, i.e., finding the silver covering.

P – Is for prayer—to God or a higher force—for quality and to be open at the time.

R – Is for relaxation by breathing profoundly and logically loosening up the large muscle groups. Tune in to music, watch an entertaining network show, drink warm milk, or appreciate a neck or foot massage.

O – Is for one thing at the time, which means the individual endeavors to stay careful and center on an unbiased action right now.

V – Is for vacation, as in taking a psychological break from a difficult circumstance by envisioning or accomplishing something lovely. This could be taking a day trip, or disregarding calls and messages for a couple of hours.

E – Is for encouragement, by conversing with oneself positively and actively to help adapt to an upsetting circumstance.

Skill No. 4: Focusing on Pros and Cons

In concentrating on advantages and disadvantages, the individual is approached to list the upsides and downsides of enduring the trouble and not taking the stress (i.e., adapting through pointless practices). It tends to be useful to recall the past results of not enduring distress and envision how it will feel to take the present trouble and dodge negative practices effectively. Through assessing the present moment and long term advantages and disadvantages, clients can comprehend the benefits of enduring pain and distress and diminish rash responses.

The distress tolerance skill is an essential tool in helping people keep up the balance, notwithstanding emergencies, instructing them to acknowledge the trouble and adapt to it in more beneficial manners. By rehearsing the skills of distracting, self-alleviating, improving the moment, and concentrating on upsides and downsides, clients can climate upsetting conditions and decrease painful feelings and destructive impulses.

Application in Dialectical Behavior Therapy

Numerous clinical psychologists assist patients in figuring out how to endure wellsprings of pain through a DBT program. DBT is a cognitive behavioral therapy that is discussion-based. There are three numerous segments to DBT; it is support-arranged, psychological based, and community. Patients of DBT normally have singular psychotherapy sessions and group sessions. The individual sessions are intended to help the patient in learning as well as improving essential social abilities. In contrast, group therapy sessions should help teach interpersonal communication, reality acceptance skills, emotional regulation, and care.

In the same way as other psychological practices, programs are patient-oriented and are created around the particular needs of every person. As a rule, therapy is intended to enable the patient to control their feelings, stress less, and endure endless wellsprings of stress. Therapy also assists patients in building social skills (mainly through gathering treatment) to help them make progressively positive relationships and circumstances for themselves later on.

Various tips, tactics, and therapies can give alleviation from visit times of extreme emotional distress. Some can be accomplished at home and all alone, while others are going to require help from a care provider. Since various conditions and distinctive biological makeups characterize each case, personalized solutions are major to long-term useful improvement. Though it might require some investment, cash, and helplessness to fabricate adequate distress tolerance, achievement can prompt unmistakable and enduring improvement in various regions over one's life.

Chapter 4 - Mindfulness

Mindfulness and Meditation for your best health in uncertain times

Regardless of what your identity is or where you're coming from, this moment in current life carries difficulties to our personal, local, and global safety and prosperity. There is no denying the present emergency influences our numerous essential needs, including our well-being, the strength of our families and our communities, the loss of occupations or salary, and even questions regarding the drawn-out direction of our social request. With this uncertainty, it is typical that we may encounter deep fear, pity, wretchedness, and misery. Our minds may take us on some dark and scary excursions.

There are also simple self-care tools we can use on an individual level to assist us in exploring mindfulness practice, not the least of which is making a mindfulness practice. Studies show that doing a regular mindfulness practice can help diminish anxiety, to rest and improve generally speaking prosperity. We are changing our relationship with the stress that can even assistance the immune system. Starting a mindfulness practice isn't troublesome, and there are numerous approaches to consolidate mindfulness into life, relying upon how much time and energy you can commit to a practice.

What is mindfulness?

Basically, "mindfulness" is the demonstration of being right now. "Mindfulness is the fundamental human capacity to be completely present, mindful of where we are and what we're doing, and not excessively responsive or overpowered by what's happening around us."

"At whatever point, you carry attention to what you're straightforwardly encountering using your faculties, or to your perspective using your thoughts and feelings, you're careful. What's more, there's developing exploration demonstrating that when you train your brain to be careful, you're renovating the physical structure of your brain."

Mindfulness practices have been around for a large number of years. Yet, present-day mindfulness became famous in the late 1970s with Jon Kabat-Zinn, a Professor of Medicine Emeritus and creator of the Stress Reduction Clinic and the Center for Mindfulness in Medicine, Health Care, and Society at the University of Massachusetts Medical School.

How would I work on being mindful?

Meditation

Meditation is a typical method to work on being mindful. There is a wide range of sorts of meditation that are drilled, yet a typical common misconception about thinking is that it is the demonstration of dispensing with thoughts from the mind. Or maybe, most meditation practices do utilize consideration of spotlight on something we can interface with utilizing our faculties, such as the breath, a sound, or words (otherwise known as a mantra: words rehashed to enable you to focus). The awareness practice is normally combined with delicately perceiving and relinquishing interruptions as they become clear.

Meditation has been utilized for a long time to reduce pressure and calm the mind with incredible achievement. Presently ongoing exploration has demonstrated potential for meditation to affect emotional processing and conceivably converse or stall brain maturing.

So for what reason doesn't everybody meditate? Meditation can be as scary as an apprentice. Realize that like anything, it requires practice and consistency. There are loads of resources accessible to start a meditation practice. I use Headspace, an application with guided meditations of various lengths—some as short as three minutes—and on various points. A quick

Google search can raise numerous resources that might be a good match for you.

Breathe

Breathing is one of the tools I discover least demanding to use for a mindful practice, particularly as a beginner. If your mind is hustling or you feel focused on, it is easy to kick back and take a deep belly breath, indeed, if you are carrying your attention and awareness to that activity, that considers being careful!

Belly breathing, AKA diaphragmatic breathing, is known to lessen the activity of the sympathetic nervous system, which produces stress hormones. Being worried in the drawn-out builds our exposure to stretch hormones and debilitates our immune system just as results in mileage on our cardiovascular framework and different pieces of our body. By working on breathing profoundly into the full limit of our rib cage, including our back rib confine, the diaphragm—the primary muscle of breathing—massages our adrenal glands and our internal organs. This delicate activity assists in resetting the nervous system into a progressively relaxed AKA parasympathetic state.

Attempt this breathing exercise for 2–3 minutes 1–2 x for each day to begin.

Lay on your back with your knees bent (or a pillow under your straight legs to help them), and a pad under your neck, so it is impartial and bolstered. You may sit in an agreeable position if you like.

Spot one hand on your stomach and one hand on your chest to screen your breath.

3. Take a couple of normal breaths in through the nose and out through the mouth. Notice which hand moves first, (tummy hand or chest hand), and how much each hand is lifted with every normal breath.

4. Deliberately take a full breath through your nose into your belly. Feel the breath move under your gut hand, let your belly rise on the breathing in, and delicately fall on the breath out.

5. Presently deliberately breathe in through your nose and direct your breath to the back of the body. Carry your attention to filling your ribcage so you can feel the rear of your ribs tenderly venture into the floor. Breathe out through the mouth, gradually, envision overwhelming pressure, uneasiness, or inconvenience, or whatever you want to give up.

6. Presently breathe into your midsection and your back rib cage. Once more, gradually breathe out. Repeat this gentle profound relaxing.

Different mindfulness ideas – attention to a moment in your

everyday practice

A fast and simple approach to practice mindfulness is to carry attention to something basic that you frequently do for the day. An ongoing model I cherished from a web recording that I tune in to was rehashing "harmony starts with me" while washing your hands–unquestionably something we are on the whole doing LOTS of nowadays! To personalize your everyday routine by picking an activity and mantra that impacts you. It very well may be anything you decided to carry attention to.

Different mindfulness ideas – attention to the movement

Mindful movement is the reason for a great deal of physical therapy. A large number of my patients have heard me state moving great is a piece of rehearsing mindfulness, and one of the essential things we as a rule practice before proceeding onward to increasingly complex movement is moving from sitting to remain with neutral poster alignment.

Be aware of how you perform simple tasks that you do every day, such as sit to stand, lifting your kid, or even how your foot accepts weight while walking. Acquire attention to your posture, day-by-day condition, such as at your work area or sit on the couch around evening time. If you end up moving or sitting in a manner that isn't perfect or doesn't feel better, don't be excessively hard on yourself, simply pause for a moment to recognize it and afterward right it.

Even though you might be investing more energy at home, ensure you continue moving. Set a clock to get up and stretch. Do some movement at standard spans like squats between conference calls, or divider sits each half-hour. If you have space and it is alright for you to do as such while social removing, walk, bicycle, run, skip, do yoga, play bring with your pooch, use the stairs–WHATEVER it is that you can do to continue moving. While you are occupied with your movement, put forth a valiant effort to remain completely present while doing it. If your mind starts to stray, recognize that, and afterward, delicately take it back to the job needing to be done.

At Cynergy, we are as yet offering physical therapy services utilizing telehealth platforms. Kindly don't stop for a second to connect with us if you are in agony or need direction in your movement. Recall that we are here for you!

Other mindfulness ideas – awareness with food

The numerous advanced performing multiple tasks tools consistently readily available combined with every one of our commitments have obscured the demonstration of being available during basic exercises of day by day living. For instance, for many of us, lunch and dinner have become an opportunity to get up to speed with desk work or messages, or even to look through different media thoughtlessly. Instead, make mealtime a device free and TV spare time for you and your family. As you eat, focus on the taste and surface of your food. I appreciate how your food smells. Take little bites and bite each chomp completely. Eat gradually, so your body has the opportunity to reveal to you it is full. Online jokes notice "the quarantine 15", and we as whole expertise stress can add to depending on nourishment for comfort. Eat when you are ravenous, not out of fatigue. Supplant careless eating with a mindful decision to rather have some herbal tea or water.

Other mindfulness ideas – develop a gratitude practice

It is simple for the brain to become involved with the negative parts of the present, particularly when we are in a position of difficult situations. Though time might be dark, every day, set aside some effort to consider a couple of things you are thankful for and record them. This can be something as straightforward as being thankful for the daylight, or as epic as getting a promotion. Research shows that routinely keeping an appreciation diary can assist us in dealing with stress, particularly when utilized related to mediation and different mindfulness skills.

Different mindfulness ideas – mindfulness for kids

Stress in adolescence can have dependable impacts. However, children have been appeared to benefit from the stress reduction of basic mindfulness exercises. Mindfulness activities for children have additionally been appeared to help control feelings and to develop confidence. The Imagine Project, Inc. has tools and tips to assist guardians in discovering ways for children to manage stress utilizing simple mindful exercises. Examples incorporate cooking together, perusing a book or drawing together, and in any event, something as simple as utilizing a singing bowl or toll at sleep time and focusing on the sound until it has wrapped up.

These are only a couple of thoughts for you to investigate if you are keen on starting a mindfulness practice. Do realize that taking little activities towards improving mindfulness can extraordinarily affect your physical, mental, and enthusiastic well-being in both the short and long term. Recollect that even only taking a full breath can affect how your body responds amid stress. Being careful requires a little exertion, yet with consideration and consistency, we would all be able to receive the benefits of this astonishing practice.

Pain is something we as a whole encounter all through our lifetime. The majority of us will hit a toe or twist an ankle and subsequently allow our bodies to rest and come back to standard life. **Chronic pain**, nonetheless, is characterized as fluctuating or reliable torment enduring over a quarter of a year, diminishing resistance to physical activity and contrarily influencing by and great personal satisfaction. The emotional and financial related cost for those influenced by chronic pain is enormous. It can influence one's capacity to work, seek after or take an interest in sentimental connections and even break point freedom in finishing basic, everyday undertakings like shopping for food or showering.

While pain can be overseen pharmacologically or remedially, contemplation and careful based treatment have experimentally demonstrated to be viable in improving physical and social capacity just as diminishing torment in those experiencing conditions like disease, various sclerosis, peripheral neuropathies, interstitial cystitis, and even diligent obscure sources. Research on mindfulness-based pressure decrease vigorously bolsters this case. One investigation, specifically, centered on those influenced by fringe neuropathy and various sclerosis. The treatment utilizing care treatment procedures included an hour and a half reflection classes every week, exhibiting amazing outcomes following two months; upon consummation, members announced diminished pain, upgrades in physical and psychological wellness, and improved resistance to physical activity.

Meditation and mindfulness-based treatment have even been appeared to build antibodies to flu and lower pressure related hormones in the blood. Additional benefits incorporate diminished degrees of anxiety and melancholy, stress decrease, improved emotions of prosperity, and capacity to focus.

When individuals come to physical therapy, they are regularly in pain and looking for help. The agony might be influencing their satisfaction and capacity to take an interest in exercises they used to take an interest in. **Stress management** and how one feels about themselves are huge parts of each recovery process. Stress management as an extra to non-intrusive treatment influences the speed and accomplishment of their recovery. Stressors influence how we feel torment, making it progressively hard to finish practices and even make it to non-intrusive therapy appointments. That is the place one of the most noteworthy advantages to contemplation as a care based therapy techniques lie: it very well may be done in any situation, in any area, with any inability, for any measure of time.

Things being what they are, how can one start meditating? If you have attempted it, you realize how hard it tends to be. Much the same as with any type of exercise, beginning with care based treatment is troublesome. While there are numerous types of meditation, most structures include concentrating on controlling our thoughts and becoming completely present concerning where we are in that specific second. This is called mindfulness.

While reading and finding out about contemplation will assist you in mindfulness therapy techniques that work for you, calm space is all you have to begin. Locate your calm space, sit in an agreeable position, and set a clock for 5, 10, 15 minutes. As far as I can tell from the first occasion when I took a stab at ruminating as a care based pressure decrease strategy, 5 minutes feels like a lifetime. Start simple and relax. Concentrate on how your breath feels, leaving the tip of your nose, and afterward entering it.

If this appears to be exceedingly challenging, which I realize it tends to be, here are some basic meditation and mindfulness therapy techniques to help you along:

Count your breath

- Tallying your breath is an incredible choice for apprentices beginning with mindfulness-based treatment. Include one on your breath, and two on your breath out. This can help calm your brain and center your considerations.
- You can include softly or in your brain. If you find that your musings have meandered, tenderly attendant you back to breathing and counting.

Visualization

- Visualization is best done by picking an ideal scene and permitting your brain to concentrate on and decorate the view. You can permit yourself to envision the hints of the scene, such as water streaming. You can allow yourself to envision the aroma noticeable all around, such as salt or rain.

- This visualization technique helps maintain your concentration and can improve the mind from meandering. It can help keep your mind occupied with your goal of easing back your considerations when clearing your brain feels too overwhelming a task.

Body Scan

- From a comfortable position, sink into your stance and carry your regard for your body. When we are in pain, we hold pressure in regions we are not deliberately mindful of.

- Starting at your toes, feel whether you're holding any strain in your feet. Focus on what your feet feel like and where they are resting. Loosen up your toes. Proceed onward to your calves, to your legs, to your glutes. Individually, focus on how they feel, where they are resting, in case you're holding any pressure in those muscles, and if you can tenderly unwind or mellow them. Proceed onward to your midsection, your lower back, your chest, and your shoulders, asking yourself similar questions. Proceed with right down your arms and hands, to your neck, jaw, and face. Scan your body and pay mind to every region, inquiring as to whether you can mellow anything else than you already have.

Mantra

- Discover a word or phrase that impacts you. It tends to be something as simple as "breathe" or something somewhat longer like "I am here." You can choose prior mantras. Whatever it is, pick something that impacts you.
- Close your eyes, breathe and rehash it to yourself again and again in your mind or discreetly softly.

Keep in mind; you can't be bad at mindfulness-based therapy. Be caring for yourself. Helping your mind is helping your body. Helping your mind will improve your rehabilitation process. Stress management as an adjunct to physical therapy will improve your results and your general quality of life.

Are You Missing Mindfulness?

The world we live in is continually pulling our regard for a million unique things at what appears to be a pace of a million miles per minute. We are bombarded with emails, text messages, social media updates, notwithstanding our various work projects, home duties, tasks, kids, and so forth. It tends to be overpowering without a doubt, also unpleasant.

While some level of stress in our lives is typical and can be profitable, chronic stress is related to various potential health problems. These can incorporate anxiety and sorrow, digestive issues, coronary illness, a sleeping disorder, weight gain, memory and concentration impairment, and muscle pain/stress. Correctly, maladaptive stress responses have been connected to the change from intense to chronic pain.

In any case, current research into is recommending that intercessions intended for advancing anxiety and stress decrease have a job in down-controlling of the effect of stress. Enter Mindfulness.

As per the American Mindfulness Research Association, mindfulness is "the state, procedure, and practice of making sure to watch moment-to-moment encounters with receptiveness and without automatic examples of recently adapted thoughts, feelings, or practices." This implies mindfulness is accessible to us in each second, should we set aside the effort to bring it into our conscious awareness. It's that thought that you may respite and take a breath as opposed to hurrying to answer your telephone, or before pushing that next bite of food into your mouth. It tends to be just simple, focusing on your breath for a second or two. You may stop and focus on different sensations: taste, hearing, pressure, or even pain, for instance. This thoughtfulness regarding the immediate sensory experience furnishes us with a chance to watch the sensation without battling to transform it smoothly. Along these lines, it very well may be advantageous in reacting to or overseeing pain. If we can isolate the physical sensation of pain from our response to it, tolerating it without judging and seeing with self-kindness, we have a recharged feeling of command over our involvement.

Mindfulness can be developed through meditation and body scans. A body examines work on planning to expand attention to the various areas of your body and experience how each part feels without attempting to transform it. Mindfulness-Based Stress Reduction (MBSR) is a research-backed research reduction program created by Jon Kabat-Zinn. It incorporates three techniques, including body, examines, sitting contemplation, just as hatha yoga practice. You should think about taking an interest in a mindful based-stress-reduction course.

But, if a course isn't an opportunity for you, there are various guided meditation applications accessible for smartphone users. Guided meditation practice is an extraordinary method to start your excursion toward grasping care and can be as short as 3-5 minutes/meeting. A couple of choices are "insight Timer" and "Headspace" to search for in the App Store.

Chapter 5 - Problem-Solving

DBT expert analysis and understanding of problems are insufficient. Hence, problem-solving strategies go outside only to be able to grasp the roots of issues and spotlight on active attempts to build up an arrangement for making change.

These strategies address explicit issues that surface in regular day-to-day existence.

The general goal is to help people with changing their behavior. In DBT, every single dysfunctional behavior is viewed as issues to be tackled. The problem solving and arrangement procedures are intended to assist individuals in getting progressively dynamic in managing issues instead of being passive or helpless.

Many people with BPD have discovered that problems are insurmountable. Accordingly, they regularly approach issues latently, or they accept they are powerless despite an issue.

If somebody presents an issue with an answer that the therapist accepts is maladaptive (suicidal, medicate use, aggression, and so forth), the therapist encourages the individual to express the issue plainly. In these cases, it's the task of the therapist and individual to work together in creating and executing new, progressively compelling answers for current issues throughout everyday life.

These solutions may incorporate learning new practices, such as how to successfully advocate for yourself, how to self-relieve, or the proper behavior inverse to a present feeling.

Finding the correct answer for anyone's problem relies upon whether the right aim and factors keeping up the problem have been resolved. You have to comprehend and acknowledge the issue and attempt to create, assess, and actualized substitute answers to be used later.

The answer to a particular issue is just convincing if it's conceivable to complete, and the individual carries out the solution.

When Life Presents You with Problems, What Are Your Options?

Solve the problem - Change the circumstance... or avoid from, leave, or escape the circumstance for good. To issue explain, you may utilize interpersonal effectiveness skills, such as walking the middle path, and additionally, you may utilize critical thinking abilities. For instance: If the problem is that you fear of flying, you could explain this by abstaining from flying. On the other hand, you could find a treatment program planned for lessening the fear of flying.

Feel better about the problem - Change (or manage) your emotional response to the issue. To feel better thinking about the difficulty, you may utilize feeling guideline abilities. For instance: Work on feeling better about having a fear of flying; then again, join a phobia support group.

Tolerate the problem - Accept and endure both the problem and your reaction to the problem. To endure the problem, you may utilize trouble resilience and mindfulness skills. For instance: If you basically can't dispose of your flying phobia and can find no real way to like it or like it, at that point, you can decrease the enduring it causes you by profoundly tolerating it: It's the thing that it's."

Remain hopeless or potentially aggravate it. To remain hopeless, you may utilize no abilities.

General Goal for DBT

To figure out how to change your practices, feelings, and thoughts that are connected to problems in living and are causing misery and distress.

SPECIFIC GOALS

Practices to Decrease:

- Mindlessness; void; being withdrawn from self as well as

other people; being judgmental

- Interpersonal conflict and stress; forlornness.

- Absence of adaptability; troubles with change.

- Up-and-down and extreme feelings; mindset ward conduct; challenges in managing feelings.

- Impulsive practices; acting without thinking; challenges are tolerating reality all things considered; tenacity; addiction.

Skills to Increase:

Mindfulness skills

Mindfulness skills assist us in concentrating attention on the current second, seeing both what's happening inside ourselves and what's happening outside of ourselves and become and remain focused. As a practice, mindfulness has become widespread, with courses instructed in companies, medical schools, and numerous different settings. Core mindfulness skills (the care "what" and "how" skills) educate us.

How to watch and experience a reality for what it's worth, to be less critical, and to live at the time with adequacy?

Mindfulness skills from a spiritual perspective (counting wise mind from a profound point of view and working on cherishing thoughtfulness) center around encountering extreme reality, framing a private association with the whole universe, and building up a feeling of opportunity. Skillful means adjusting doing mind and being the brain and insightful mind by walking the middle path.

Interpersonal effectiveness skills. Interpersonal effectiveness skills assist us in keeping up and improve relationships both with individuals we are close to and with outsiders. Core interpersonal effectiveness skills show us how to manage conflict situations, to get what we need and need, and to disapprove of undesirable demands and requests—this in a way that keeps up our dignity and others' preferring and regard for us. Building relationships and ending destructive relationship skills empower us to find potential companions, get individuals to like us, and keep up positive associations with others. They also tell the best way to manufacture closeness with others from one perspective and cut off damaging associations on the other. Walking the middle path skills help us in our relationships, offsetting acknowledgment with a change in ourselves and our associations with others.

Emotion regulation skills. Emotion regulation incorporates improving control of feelings, even though complete emotional control can't be accomplished. To a certain extent, we are what our identity is, and emotionality is a piece of us. In any case, we can gain more power and maybe figure out how to tweak a few feelings. Understanding and naming emotion skills empower us to comprehend feelings when all is said in done and comprehend and distinguish our feelings. Changing emotional responses skills help us lessen the force of difficult or undesirable feelings (anger, sadness, shame, and so on), and change circumstances that brief excruciating or unwanted emotions. Reducing vulnerability to feeling mind abilities empower us to decrease weakness in turning out to be incredibly or painfully emotional, and to increase emotional resilience. Overseeing truly difficult feelings abilities help us to acknowledge continuous feelings and to manage extreme emotions.

Distress tolerance skills. Distress tolerance is the ability to endure and endure crises without exacerbating the situation. These skills show us how to acknowledge and completely go into a real existence that may not be the existence we sought after or need. Crisis survival skills empower us to endure painful events, inclinations, and feelings when we can't improve things immediately.

Acceptance skills license us to diminish enduring by tolerating and carrying on with a real existence that isn't the existence we need. When the crisis is an addiction, skills empower us to withdraw from addiction and carry on with the existence of forbearance. Chain analysis and missing-link analysis skills are approaches to figure out the reasons for issue practices and plan for problem-solving.

Chapter 6 - Addictions

Addiction is a complex condition, a brain disease that is showed by impulsive substance use, notwithstanding an uncertain outcome. Individuals with addiction (serious substance use disorder) have an excellent spotlight on utilizing a certain substance (s, such as alcohol or medications, to the point that it assumes control over their life. They continue utilizing alcohol or medication when they realize it will cause problems. However, various compelling medicines are accessible, and individuals can recuperate from enslavement and lead normal, gainful lives.

Individuals can build up a dependence on:

- Alcohol

- Marijuana

- PCP, LSD and different psychedelic drugs

- Inhalants, such as paint thinners and glue

- Opioid pain killers, such as codeine and oxycodone, heroin

- Narcotics, hypnotics, and anxiolytics (drugs for nervousness, such as tranquilizers)

- Cocaine, methamphetamine and different stimulants

- Tobacco

Individuals with substance use disorder have twisted thinking, conduct, and body capacities. Changes in the brain's wiring cause individuals to have extraordinary desires for the medication and make it difficult to quit utilizing the medication. Brain imaging examines show changes in the regions of the mind that identify with judgment, dynamic, learning, memory, and behavioral control.

These substances can cause harmful changes in how the brain functions. These progressions can keep going long after the quick impacts of the medication—the intoxication. Intoxication is the serious delight, quiet, expanded faculties, or a high brought about by the medication. Intoxication indications are diverse for every substance.

After some time, individuals with addiction develop tolerance, which means they need a larger amount to feel the impacts.

As per the National Institute on Drug Abuse, individuals start ingesting medications for an assortment of reasons, including:

- To feel better - feeling of pleasure, "high"

- To feel good - e.g., reduce stress

- To improve - improve performance

- Curiosity and peer pressure

Individuals with addictive disorders might know about their concern yet cannot stop it regardless of whether they need to. The addiction may mess wellbeing up just as issues at work and with relatives and companions. The misuse of drugs and alcohol is the main source of preventable ailments and premature death.

Side effects of substance use disorder are assembled into four classifications:

- Impaired control: a craving or compelling impulse to utilize the substance; want or failed endeavors to chop down or control substance use.

- Social problems: substance use makes disappointment complete significant tasks at work, school, or home; social; work or relaxation exercises are surrendered or decreased given substance use.

- Unsafe use: the substance is utilized in risky settings; proceeded with use regardless of known issues.

- Drug impacts: resilience (a requirement for bigger add up to get a similar impact); withdrawal side effects (diverse for every substance).

Numerous individuals experience both dysfunctional behavior and addiction. The psychological sickness might be available before the addiction. However, the compulsion may trigger or aggravate a mental disorder worse.

How Is Addiction Treated?

Compelling medicines for addiction are accessible.

The initial step making a course for recuperation is an acknowledgment of the issue. The recovery process can be obstructed when an individual denies having a problem and needs an understanding of substance misuse and addiction. The mediation of concerned loved ones regularly prompts treatment.

A health professional can lead to a proper evaluation of side effects to check whether a substance use issue exists. Regardless of whether the issue appears to be extreme, a great many people with a substance use issue can profit by treatment. Sadly, numerous individuals who could profit by treatment don't get help.

Since addiction influences numerous parts of an individual's life, different sorts of treatment are regularly required. For most, a mix of medication and individual or gathering treatment is best. Treatment moves toward addressing a person's circumstance, and any co-happening clinical, mental, and social problems can prompt continued recuperation.

Medications are used to control cravings for peace of mind and to relieve extreme withdrawal symptoms. Treatment can help dependent people comprehend their behavior and inspirations, create higher confidence, adapt to pressure, and address other mental health problems. Treatment may include:

- Hospitalization
- Therapeutic communities (exceptionally controlled, tranquilize free conditions) or calm houses
- Outpatient programs

Numerous individuals get self-help groups for people (Alcoholics Anonymous, Narcotics Anonymous) just as their relatives (Al-Anon or Nar-Anon Family Groups) valuable.

Dialectical Abstinence

For individuals searching for help with substance abuse, there are numerous choices with different ways of thinking and ways to deal with treatment. One alternative that is regularly disregarded is dialectical behavior therapy (DBT). When may an individual with substance abuse consider DBT as a practical choice?

Dialectical behavioral therapy is settled as a powerful treatment for individuals with borderline personality disorder just as depression and anxiety. Less notable is DBT's viability in helping individuals overcome addiction.

How DBT approaches substance abuse

DBT targets enslavement as an indication of feeling dysregulation. When an individual encounters feelings as very intense, and experiences issues enduring painful emotions, the person may look to substances or other addictive practices as a technique for adapting. Individuals whose substance abuse is identified with overseeing feelings may profit by DBT. Those whose issues are less extreme may do well with less intensive treatment.

Since DBT offers a strong aptitude preparing program for individuals who experience difficulty overseeing severe feelings, it has been seen as valuable in helping individuals supplant addictive practices with reliable adapting methodologies.

DBT for substance misuse has a few contrasts contrasted with standard DBT. These distinctions in the treatment are intended to represent one of a kind needs of individuals with addictions.

DBT's use of dialectical abstinence

In the treatment of addictions, for quite some time, there has been a separation between the individuals who advance restraint and the individuals who promote harm options. As opposed to looking only at both of these alternatives, DBT's approach is to help "dialectical abstinence." This implies that the therapist helps the individual with the treatment to do everything conceivable to accomplish the goal while also supporting a damage decrease approach when backslide occurs. This dialectical stance permits the individual to get the advantages of both approaches.

DBT for substance abuse has a few contrasts contrasted with standard DBT. These distinctions in the treatment are intended to represent the special needs of individuals with addictions.

In light of DBT's balance of endeavors toward change and endeavors toward acknowledgment, individuals are upheld in quickly and for all-time, halting the utilization of substances, at the same time being urged to progress in the direction of the desired goal if, when backslide happens. While numerous substance abuse medicines require total restraint to receive services, DBT adopts an alternate approach. Individuals must remain focused on the goal of forbearance, yet also get backing to refocus if a relapse happens.

The DBT treatment structure

Individual DBT therapists can treat addiction through a focus on center around substance-related behaviors. Since DBT sessions are exceptionally organized around typically explicit focuses on, the therapist will explicitly address practices that are connected to substance use-related results. These targets frequently incorporate diminishing utilization of illegal substances, mitigating physical distress, lessening yearnings and inclinations to utilize, and avoid circumstances and signs related to drug use.

DBT additionally utilizes a lot of strategies known as community enforcement. Community reinforcement is a method that expands social help for abstinence from substance use.

In the DBT skills training group, abilities for conquering addictions are remembered for the distress tolerance section; these incorporate abilities to get ready for dialectical abstinence, an overview of behavioral patterns that show when one is in an "addict mind" or "clear mind," the community enforcement model, other rebellion, and more. These abilities are expected to assist individuals in strengthening non-addictive practices and end addiction-linked behaviors.

Considering DBT as a treatment option

A few inquiries to consider in assessing DBT as a treatment option for substance abuse include:

- Is the addictive behavior connected to a problem managing emotional ups and down?
- Is the individual resolved to finish and permanent abstinence as a goal, yet needing abilities to move in the direction of it?
- Would the individual benefit from an intensive, organized treatment that incorporates week by week individual therapy and a skills group?

If the appropriate responses are affirmative, an evaluation for DBT may help.

In looking for DBT as a treatment option, it's imperative to locate an authorized clinician who is seriously prepared in the treatment the person in question is offering, and who offers complete DBT (individual therapy, skills training, telephone instructing, and cooperation in a consultation team). In the wake of finding a provider, you can get some information about their training and services advertised.

Dialectical Abstinence vs. Harm Reduction

Two of the primary addiction recovery strategies utilized when treating drug addicts and heavy drinkers are restraint and harm reduction. While proponents of the two strategies tout high achievement rates, they endeavor to expose the adequacy of the other through investigations, medical research papers, and various statistics. It's essential to think about the harm reduction model versus the abstinence model. At Behavioral Health of the Palm Beaches, we are doing only that.

Abstinence Defined

When contrasting harm reduction versus abstinence, you have to look at each independently to begin initially. Abstinence is characterized as the total suspension of medication or alcohol use. Drug and alcohol abstinence has, for some time, been proclaimed as the best approach to conquer fixation. In any event, going back hundreds of years, before addictions were treated as medical conditions, the traditional method to break medication or alcohol conditions was through abstinence.

Presently known as the Minnesota Model, abstinence addiction treatment (which was initially made to enable an individual to detox from alcohol yet is currently used to treat all addictions) depends on 10 essential tenets.

- The first tenet is that alcohol habit is an involuntary and primary disease and essential sickness. It's viewed as describable and diagnosable.

- Alcoholism ought to be viewed as a dynamic and chronic disease.

- While this disease can't be completely relieved, it very well may be overseen.

- While a few people are pretty much spurred to get residential alcohol treatment, this doesn't characterize the accomplishment of the treatment outcome.

- Holistic addiction treatment for alcoholism ought to be utilized. This strategy will address the physical, mental, social, and profound measurements.

- A fruitful alcoholic treatment plan ought to incorporate the alcoholic being treated with deference and nobility.

- Heavy drinkers and addicts are powerless against the maltreatment of a wide range of temperament changing medications, and these issues ought to be tended to during treatment.

- Addiction ought to be treated by a group of multi-disciplinary professionals. The best treatment will include increasingly casual, closer connections between the experts and the patients.

- The primary counselors will be one of the most significant elements of the treatment. The individual in question ought to be a comparable segment to the patient and maybe a previous addicted also. This ought to advance a domain of self-revelation, common recognizable proof, and mutual support.

- The best treatment for alcoholism incorporates a direction to Alcoholics Anonymous (AA). These standards incorporate gathering support, set desires, and individual directing.

Minnesota Model

In the late 1940s, the yet fledgling addiction recovery treatment industry was at a misfortune about how to manage heavy drinkers. They were already jailed, put in organizations for the intellectually sick, or left to the destiny of their addictions. At that point, however, AA's membership had developed to more than 90,000, and it had demonstrated to be fairly effective in improving alcoholics.

The production of AA in 1935, trailed by distributing its essential content, "The Big Book," combined with a few clinical advances gradually prompted the acknowledgment of alcoholism as a disease, which was a forerunner to the Minnesota Model. In the United States, Minnesota Model or similar abstinence just projects involve roughly 96% of all addiction treatments.

Made in 1949, Minnesota Model previously spread to the then little, not-revenue driven association called the Hazelden

Foundation (presently the Hazelden Betty Ford Foundation) and afterward immediately arrived at each side of the nation? This approach (which has since stretched out past only treatment for alcoholism) accepts that the illness of addiction has become so solid inside a person that the individual in question can't have a solitary taste of a mixed drink without gambling total backslide.

Made in 1949, Minnesota Model previously spread to the then little, not-revenue driven association called the Hazelden Foundation (presently the Hazelden Betty Ford Foundation) and afterward immediately arrived at each side of the nation. This approach (which has since stretched out past only treatment for alcoholism) expects that the ailment of enslavement has become so solid inside a person that the person can't have an individual taste of a mixed refreshment without gambling total backslide.

When looking at harm reduction vs. abstinence, it's additionally critical to raise the AA Model. Abstinence depends on AA standards, which use otherworldliness and family inclusion as an establishment of its lessons. The Minnesota Model adjusted the initial five stages of AA and included clinical and psychological segments. Patients are commonly required to go to AA meetings following treatment in the Minnesota Model.

The First Five Steps of the AA Model Translated:

Concede Powerlessness: We conceded we were feeble over our dependence–that our lives had gotten unmanageable. In the Minnesota Model, this progression serves to make someone who is addicted to survey their substance use history and recognize the unsafe outcomes that have followed subsequently.

Discover Hope: We came to accept that power more noteworthy than we could reestablish us to mental soundness. With the spirituality viewpoint expelled, this converts into "there's help if you need to make a difference."

Give up: We settled on a choice to give our will and our lives to the consideration of God. Under the Minnesota Model, this implies the fanatic must quit settling on choices in the way the person in question has before. It implies taking advice from others and letting them help you.

Take Inventory: We made a looking and courageous good stock of ourselves. This starts the procedure of self-pardoning and self-acknowledgment, even despite all the damage substance abuse has caused.

Offer Inventory: We admitted to God, to ourselves, and another person, the specific idea of our wrongs. Similarly, as one needs to excuse themselves, it's imperative to look for absolution from others.

Harm Reduction Therapy Defined

When comparing harm reduction versus abstinence, you will rapidly see that hurt decrease for liquor and medications is altogether different from forbearance. The mischief decrease the way to deal with dependence treatment alludes to two separate thoughts. The first is to diminish the well-being, social, and financial damage related to medication or liquor use, without lessening the mishandling substance's genuine utilization. This methodology has been advanced in European nations since the 1980s when government authorities were scanning for approaches to battle the developing HIV epidemic. Needle exchange programs and methadone medicines were conceived from this approach.

The other type of harm reduction suggests diminished use of medications or alcohol. This style of harm reduction disputably came into vogue in the mid-90s with the making of the Moderation Management association established by Audrey Kishline. A self-recognized issue consumer herself, Kishline didn't have faith in the sickness theory or principles educated by the AA.

She made Moderation Management as an elective way to abstinence treatment. This program permits consumers to keep expending liquor with some restraint. The association scorned the need to submit to God or any higher otherworldly force, something that was transparently invited by people who weren't strict and maybe put off by constrained otherworldliness.

Harm reduction centers around self-responsibility and, similar to AA, use meetings, peer support, and online services to self-report alcohol use. In principle, this permits drunkards to monitor their drinking.

Moderation Management as an association lost a great deal of validity when Kishline conceded in January 2000 that her drinking issues were too serious to even think about being overseen by moderation, and she entered AA. Lamentably, two months after her affirmation, she drove an alcoholic and killed a father and his children in a horrendous vehicle accident.

While harm reduction is as yet polished in certain areas in the country, it has lost great energy and isn't exceptionally used. Harm reduction strategy is fundamentally proposed for consumers who haven't yet had their lives altogether harmed by abuse (which means they have not lost positions, demolished relationships, obliterated their wellbeing, or experienced legal problems thus).

Inspecting Success Rates of Harm Reduction vs. Abstinence Treatment

While talking about either abstinence treatment or the harm reduction approach, finding a solid and precise achievement rate is almost inconceivable. This is mainly because the collection of this data depends entirely on patients self-revealing their alcohol or medication use. With the shame and stigma connected to dependence, particularly following often expensive treatment, some recuperating addicts may not be inevitable or legit in conceding slips or relapses.

Alcoholics Anonymous A has spared incalculable lives and has undeniably been fruitful in changing the lives of numerous alcohol abusers and their families. Yet, their revealed achievement rates run somewhere in the range of 5% to 70%, contingent upon the wellspring of the data. The equivalent can be said for most abstinence-only programs.

With regards to moderation, since the meaning of accomplishment and disappointment appears to be foggy, the best-case scenario, a considerable lot of the measurements connected to the strategy, are additionally temperamental. How can one characterize achievement in this model? Going from six drinks for each week to five? Decreasing down to two drinks for each month? This subjective nature makes it a lot simpler to guarantee achievement in harm reduction than in abstinence.

Here are a few measurements from past examinations into the efficacies of abstinence versus harm reduction.

- A 2006 Scottish investigation followed 695 recouping alcoholics for 33 months following treatment. The outcomes demonstrated that simply 5.9% of women and 9% of men had remained abstinent for if 90 days during the close to three-year stretch.

- Thirty-four percent of people who stay abstinent for one-to-three years will wind up relapsing. That number dives to 14% when people stay abstinent for five years.

- Roughly 30% of Moderation Management members proceed onward to restraint just programs.

- In 2012, 50% of counselors met in an examination said that it was alright for alcohol abusers to have an infrequent drink.

Criticisms of Harm Reduction Therapy

A great part of the abstinence reduction recuperation community attacks the damage decrease hypothesis for empowering addicts to keep drinking. They see this as a reason for relapse. As was found with Kishline (it was later discovered that she was concealing her drinking the whole time), it's normal for an individual to lie about how much alcohol the person in question is devouring. The mission statement of Moderation Management could be seen as an avocation to drink.

MM enables people to accept personal responsibility regarding picking and keeping up their way, regardless of whether moderation and abstinence. MM promotes early self-acknowledgment of unsafe drinking conduct when moderation is all the more effectively attainable goal.

Since Moderation Management groups are not planned to be long-term or serious, enrollment is prevalently online, and groups don't frame effectively or keep going long. This is in direct differentiation to AA, which routinely includes groups with individuals who have been calm for a considerable length of time or even decades. When a person attempts to make a MM meeting, they should make the game plans all alone (space, time, rewards, enrolling individuals, and so on) and risk losing secrecy, which might be an issue for prominent individuals.

Maybe the most significant criticism of damage decrease is that it does not hold a lot of weight when managing illegal substances, such as heroin or cocaine. How can one suggest doing less heroin, precious crystal meth, or cocaine as a treatment procedure? A single episode of binge drinking can be possibly fatal; however, it's less inclined to be deadly than when utilizing heroin. In 2013, of the 38 million conceded binge drinkers in the U.S., there were just 2,200 deaths because of alcohol poisoning. Around the same time, 8,260 people kicked the bucket from heroin overdoses.

This equivalent issue reaches out to painkiller addictions since harm reduction does not utilize treatments that would instruct patients on the best way to deal with their pain without the utilization of drugs.

Criticisms of Abstinence-Only Treatments

The most widely recognized prosecution against abstinence-based addiction recovery ways of thinking is their severe adherence to the 12-steps model, which centers on religious habit treatment. Not all human beings are alright with imploring or concentrating on otherworldliness. Opponents of the strategy aim to low achievement rates and a reluctance for some people to look for treatment since they would prefer not to stop utilizing totally.

- Around 10% of individuals who need treatment for a substance misuse issue look for and get it.

- Joined data from 2010 to 2013 shows that 24.5% of the individuals who required addiction treatment didn't prepare it referred to as not being to stop using.

Do numerous addicts struggle with the idea? Of putting down their substance of decision until the end of time. Others contend that the abstinence just system unjustifiably slanders addicts who relapse and propagates the negative stigma related to addiction. Another issue non-supporters raise about forbearance just projects is that they center exclusively on drunkards who have built up a physical reliance. This procedure overlooks "problem drinkers" whose use has not yet arrived at damaging levels. As indicated by the National Institute on Alcohol Abuse and Alcoholism, 16% of the grown-up populace is non-subordinate issue drinkers. A report from the Centers from Disease Control and Prevention demonstrated that nine out of 10 binge drinkers weren't alcohol dependent.

Conversation and Recommendations of Harm Reduction vs. Abstinence Treatment

The contention between harm reduction and abstinence comes down to a person's needs. For an individual who is an analyzed drunkard or an overwhelming consumer (over 5 drinks on a similar event on every one of at least five days in a 30-day time frame), harm reduction may not be a practical choice. It depends on an individual who recently experienced issues controlling their toasting unexpectedly create discretion. The same amount of addiction therapists would confirm that this is an unreasonable expectation.

Alcoholics and medication addicts generally require something beyond the standard 30-day detox recommended by Moderation Management and other damage decrease associations. Also, they require long-term alcohol and medication recovery that incorporates directing and other therapeutic services. A great part of the clinical network arranges dependence as a ceaseless mind infection. Abstinence treatment is the best way to guarantee that the ailment stays disappearing.

Consumers who self-recognized as expecting to check their drinking may see harm reduction as a superior technique. It's less serious, more affordable, less intrusive, and doesn't close the entryway on socially drinking. It does, in any case, require a degree of restraint and responsibility that is extraordinary in problem drinkers. What number of consumers can even review what number of mixed drinks they had the earlier night? How sensible is it for a consumer to delay in the middle of beverages and discounts on a note pad when the person in question has consumed a beverage?

Families endeavoring to discover substance abuse treatment for a friend or family member should sincerely survey the monstrosity of the issue. If an individual is abusing illegal medications or doctor-prescribed medications, abstinence just treatment might be prudent. In like manner, if an individual has done huge harm to their life or the lives of others, abstinence just treatment is the most advisable course of action. Nonetheless, a person who is only a "problem drinker" who has not endured significant outcomes because of drinking might be effective with a harm reduction approach.

Chapter 7 - Building a Satisfying Life

Each life merits living, yet a few of us discover our lives uninspiring, unpleasant, or even hopeless. Life is all the more fulfilling when we create schedules that incorporate unsurprising and pleasant unwinding and fun offset with obligations.

Schedules shouldn't be complicated. The vast majority of us benefit from careful simplicity throughout everyday life. Mindful simplicity implies interfacing with and encountering the normal that characterizes and structures our days.

Responsibilities

We get overpowered when our duties are not dealt with day by day. Break bigger duties into day by day steps. Make a list of both major and minor responsibilities.

Progressing Structure

Schedules are about structure that is progressing, unsurprising, and rehashing. Structure shields us from stalling out in our symptoms and is the establishment for building a wonderful life.

Utilization of Skills

Recall that you have to learn and practice the entirety of your abilities as a piece of your daily schedule, much the same as somebody in school or school does homework. Incorporate updates for the skills you explicitly need to rehearse on a particular day. Additionally, recall different abilities may be expected to follow your daily practice, such as opposite to Emotion.

Traditions

Traditions offer importance to our lives and those of others. Some portion of a fulfilling life is creating traditions that you and the individuals around you appreciate. A significant number of us think traditions as attached to occasions and seasons, and those can be enjoyable to set up. Yet, traditions can be as basic as a family bowling nights.

Interests Included

Schedules that do exclude our advantages are hard to keep up. Make certain to work in what you like to do. Make sure to move toward another intrigue or action with a Non-judgmental stance.

Novelty

Be mindful so as not to incorporate an excessive amount of structure with your everyday practice. Schedules additionally need space for adaptability. Ensure you unequivocally leave space to attempt new exercises or to be unconstrained. Think about booking a free morning, evening, night, or day into your everyday practice.

Imagine a Satisfying Life

Schedules, timetables, and structure set aside some effort to get set up. Recall not to abandon building propensities toward carrying on with an additionally fulfilling life. Remain aware of how your routine will assist you in your needs, goals, and qualities. Try not to surrender!

Bringing DBT Skills out of Treatment and Into Everyday Life

If the challenge of living with the side effects of Borderline Personality Disorder (BPD) has gotten too hard even to consider regularly facing, looking for help at a Borderline Personality Disorder treatment focus might be the next stage.

At a BPD treatment center, you will learn Dialectical Behavior Therapy (DBT) skills that will assist you in bettering deal with your BPD side effects. You will learn DBT skills in group sessions and practice them for the day, both in individual DBT treatment and with individuals from your treatment team.

A Borderline Personality Disorder treatment focuses, in any case, in this present reality. At a BPD treatment center, mainly a special BPD treatment focus, you're encircled by other people who comprehend what it's to manage the anxiety, the fear of relinquishment, the unstable relationships, and the bothering feeling that nobody "gets" you.

You're guided via trained DBT therapists who are patient and ready to work through your challenges with you. This may not generally be the situation when you're in your regular day to day existence.

Utilizing the skills learned in Dialectical Behavior Therapy at a treatment place is unique about taking these abilities with you again into the outside world. So how would you make the change?

Utilizing DBT Skills in Everyday Life

Here are some different things you can do to assist you in practicing and coordinate Dialectical Behavior Therapy skills into your regular daily existence:

Realize the power of the example you are setting. With the skills you presently have in your "tool belt," you can stop a circumstance that, as far as you can tell, may have spun uncontrollably wild. If a colleague or adored one is becoming annoyed or encountering disappointment, staying cool and present can diffuse whatever is causing the issue. You don't have to verbalize or share your skills. Your vitality will say a lot.

Take a few minutes for yourself for the day. Discover time to step away and intellectually reconnect with your goals and the means you have taken to contact them.

Recognize that your DBT skills have enabled you to ensure yourself without being aggressive or defensive. These positive skills experience supplanted the previous difficulty causing the go-to defense mechanism.

Venture out of the mental side of your training and focus on your physical self. In any event once per day, accomplish something physical: go for a walk, hit the gym, or practice yoga. This can ease the heat off the language of DBT skills (words like modules, approval, all the abbreviations, and so forth) that might be swirling through your head and simply let the abilities sink into your being.

At long last, when searching for a DBT treatment focus, discover one that offers a continuum of care. If you're entering private DBT treatment, find a Dialectical Behavior Therapy treatment program that gives a full continuum of care, including day treatment and outpatient DBT treatment. That way, you can start joining the DBT abilities you learn into regular daily existence while still getting help.

3 DBT Skills Everyone Can Benefit From

Dialectical behavioral therapy (DBT) is a profoundly successful kind of cognitive-behavioral (CBT), initially made to treat borderline personality disorder. Today, it's used to treat an assortment of conditions, such as bipolar disorder, eating disorder, and depression. DBT shows clients four arrangements of behavioral skills: mindfulness, distress tolerance; interpersonal effectiveness; and feeling guidelines.

Mindfulness

As indicated by Van Dijk, mindfulness signifies "carrying on with your life more right now, rather than permitting yourself to be captured by the past and what's to come." By practicing mindfulness, we become mindful of our thoughts, emotions, activities, and responses. We're ready to stop, check-in, recognize our feelings, and deliberately settle on sound choices.

To rehearse this skill, Van Dijk proposed taking a walk carefully. "Feel your body as it strolls, and notice how it just realizes what it needs to do to move each convoluted arrangement of muscles to accomplish the goal of walking." Pay thoughtfulness regarding the shade of the sky, the trees you're passing, and what the houses resemble, she said.

If your mind meanders, divert it to the current second. You may decide to pull together on your outer experience: what's going on around you. However, you may pull together on your inner experience: your contemplations, feelings, and physical sensations. Here the key is to see what you're encountering without becoming involved with it.

Such as in case you're snared in your contemplations, this resembles: "Susan is extremely decent. She's such an extraordinary individual. I want to be increasingly similar to her. I ought to inquire as to whether she needs to go for coffee at some point. I'd prefer to become more acquainted with her better." Instead, watching your contemplations resembles: "There's an idea that Susan is such a decent individual... "

Reality Acceptance

This ability centers on tolerating our day by day encounters and attempting to acknowledge the more excruciating occasions that have occurred. Since fighting reality just uplifts our affliction.

Such as as indicated, you're sitting in a work meeting, exhausted insane. You begin considering the various things you could be doing. Rather than letting yourself know, "I have such a great amount of stuff to do; this is a misuse of my time!" you remind yourself: There's no other option for me. This is something I need to endure. What will be? Relax."

She shared these extra models: You have to rush home. However, you're getting each red light. Rather than getting baffled, you take a full breath and ask yourself: "What will be. I'll return home when I arrive."

You have to top off your car. However, gas costs have soared. Once more, you inhale profoundly, and state to yourself: "There's no way around it. I need gas. Blowing up won't help."

You need to stroll to work because your vehicle is in the shop. It's not far, yet it's pouring. You take a full breath and state: "It's simply downpour. I'll bring a towel, and I'll get dry when I get the chance to work."

Non-judgmental Stance

This skill addresses being less judgmental when all is said in done. Van Dijk proposed beginning to see when you judge things as positive or negative. Negative decisions will, in general, lift our emotional pain. So when you're irate, aggravated or frustrated, focus on what judgment you're making, she said. At that point, center on supplanting that judgment with reality and other feelings you have.

Van Dijk shared these models: Instead of "the climate is awful today," you state, "it's coming down at the beginning of today, and I'm disturbed because I need to stroll to work." Instead of saying, "you're an awful friend," you state: "There have been a couple of times as of late when you've dropped plans with me, at last, to go out with another person. Furthermore, I feel hurt and angry about this."

Rather than saying, "My partner is an idiot," you state: "I have been working extended periods, and when I returned home the previous evening, my accomplice approached me what I was making for supper. I felt extremely irate about this and disillusioned that he is not putting forth an attempt to assist."

Being less judgmental does not wipe out our pain. However, it helps us lessen feelings, such as anger. "[A] and in doing so, we're ready to think all the more plainly and astutely, opening-up decisions for us [such as] 'would I like to burn through effort being angry at this individual?'" It enables us to issue unravel, and once more, settle on choices that serve and bolster us.

Such as she took her computer to get fixed. After she got it, she understood that imperative presentations and archives were absent. For reasons unknown, the individual didn't back up her C: drive since he thought she spared everything under "documents." Understandably, fantastically disturbed. Yet, she took a full breath, and as opposed to shouting and condemning him, she asked what they could do.

"It probably won't get unraveled. Yet, passing judgment on him is just going to enhance my outrage, and I simply would prefer not to burn through the effort on that." She was additionally pleased with how she took care of the circumstance, which supported her confidence. What's more, it didn't raise her circulatory strain or trigger other physical issues.

Once more, we all can profit by getting progressively mindful of our thoughts and emotions, tolerating what is, and being less judgmental of ourselves as well as other people. Without a doubt, these are skills that lead to a more useful life.

Chapter 8 - Social Media

Do you know somebody who does not have social media? I'm speculating that I know the response to that question, and I'm exceptionally blameworthy of fiddling with practically every online life account out there also! Why? Since its fun, diverting, and invigorating. Americans are said to go through 4.7 hours on our telephones every day, all the more explicitly, Americans are accounted for to look into the social average and normal of 17 times each day. That implies we check at any rate social media account once consistently. Online networking has a staggering method of causing us to feel acknowledged and dismissed all simultaneously, particularly when we are carelessly exploring records and making a decision about others as "great," "bad," "appalling," "beautiful," and so on. Judgment is a characteristic human reaction as it encourages us to comprehend the world and put encounters into classifications. Decisions, particularly comparisons, also can disentangle us so that that causes us to feel inferior, unloved, and unworthy.

While instructing DBT abilities class one night, I chose to have my class do an experiment where everybody was approached to open up a social media account and carefully look through the feed, simply seeing the thoughts and feelings that come up. It caused me a deep sense of shock; there was not one impartial or positive remark saw by the class; they all saw their harsh comparisons and negative self-talk. Since the time that test, I have attempted to turn out to be increasingly mindful of the individual effect that internet based life has on me. Try not to misunderstand me; I'm in no way, shape, or form pushing for online networking to be discarded because it has such a large number of extraordinary limits. I essentially promise myself and all others to do a couple of basic things to make the odds of a positive online life experience increasingly feasible. First of all, have a go at constraining your time spent on a record to close to 20 minutes. Second, be aware of your correlations with others and negative self-talk. Thirdly, make a point to adjust your online time with up close and personal communication. These are a couple of basic strides to guarantee that you don't get dependent on social media. After all, it's called "social" media and planned to be fun and add association with our lives; it's not intended to include more pain. So we should assume responsibility for social media and not let it assume responsibility for us!

How to Manage Social Media Anxiety

Are Snapchat, Instagram, Facebook, and Twitter, causing your high teen to feel anxious or discouraged? Your child or little girl isn't the only one. Late investigations and overviews uncover that social media is one contributing component towards rising psychological well-being issues among teenagers. An expansion in young people's powerlessness to sleep, loneliness, and pain started around a similar time that the first iPhone was discharged. Shockingly, it's anything but an occurrence.

Teenagers who utilize social media for a considerable length of time every day will, in general, feel increasingly anxious, progressively shaky, and all the more alone. However, social media isn't the main source of diminished psychological wellness. Run of the mill teenager issues, similar to social and scholarly weights, additionally add to these genuinely normal emotions. What's most significant is helping your child adapt to overpowering feelings—regardless of the source.

There's certainly not a "one size fits all" way to deal with child-rearing adolescents with social media related anxiety. Much the same as teenagers utilize social media in different manners for various purposes, there are various ways for parents to help their kids. Here are some useful procedures to consider:

To begin with, focus on when your child appears to be disappointed, pushed, or furious about social media. Does your adolescent become on edge when posting photographs of oneself? Does your teenager get irritated when the person in question sees recordings of their companions hanging out without him/her? Notice when social media is setting off these emotions. Make certain to observe what part of social media is most activating for your teenager.

At that point, set up an open conversation with your teen about their social media use and how it could be contrarily affecting the person in question. Check-in with your teen—particularly when you notice that the person in question is upset. When conversing with your teen, approve how the person feels. Show that you comprehend where the individual in question is originating from and how testing things can be. What's more, offer to listen carefully and work through your teen's issues together.

Abstain from adopting a win or bust strategy with regards to social media. By removing your teen's telephone, you may make more clash in the process instead of tending to the current issue. Consider that expelling the device keeps teens from utilizing the parts of social media that they appreciate. Rather, work with your teen to set sans screen times. You may have sans screen time during supper and an hour or two preceding bed, for instance. Your teen may need to attempt a without screen end of the week from time to time. Structure and arrangement that you and your child or little girl can both concur on.

With academic, social, and computerized pressures for teens, it's no big surprise that psychological well-being issues continue expanding. As a parent, you can be there for your teen by helping the person address social media related stressors and discover arrangements together. Urge your teen to assume responsibility for their advanced propensities, so the person in question can have a sound, improved relationship with technology.

BPD, DBT, and Facebook

You mustn't have BPD for the widely inclusive social media time suck to cause you to feel discouraged. A recent report established that the more you use Facebook, the less fulfilled you become with your own life. There's a lot of episodic proof that is valid–how often have you look the photos of your companions' get-away, new houses, and $3000 Pottery Barn dining room tables, and chided yourself for not winning more cash? How often have you perused notices like, "happy anniversary to my astonishing, flawless spouse, who treats me like sovereignty and gets me flowers each day," and accepted it must be the shortcoming that you're despite everything single?

Does it cause me to feel unimportant when I conceal these individuals from my feed? Sure. It also causes me to feel like I may have the option to make some writing done that day, rather than slithering behind the couch with a bucket of sesame noodles as well as benzos.

Nonetheless, there's nothing more awful about Facebook–particularly for those of us who should have "abandonment issues" inked over our foreheads–than sending somebody a message or companion demand and being overlooked. Of course, I think about the "Other" folder. I also think about the godforsaken "Seen" notifications.

If you have BPD, there's no social media connection all the more activating (and I hate that word, however it applies here) than sending somebody a message, seeing that they've seen it, and hearing nothing back. As of late, I informed another writer, one whose work I love, to reveal to her I was expounding on one of her books. Not simply in my journal, either–I was expounding on it for a professional publication that was paying me. We have a mutual friend, so I sent her a friend request.

In no time, I saw the abhorrent dim "seen" underneath my message. She didn't responded back, and she didn't acknowledge my friend's request for about fourteen days.

I struggled. I got some information about her, and my companion stated, "Gracious, she's extremely decent!" So following a 14-day holding up period just marginally less upsetting than a mid-'90s HIV test, I thought of her back, referenced our companion, and revealed to her I'd be regarded if she'd acknowledge my friend's request.

It was "seen" after 20 minutes. Also, I got nothing.

I know that contemplating what I got or didn't get is one of those hindered in-childhood phenomena that drove me into dialectical behavior therapy in any case. I know it's not about me. I realize others have lives and issues, and that Facebook is, as the well-known (and frequently shared) axiom goes, "such as contrasting yours in the background with another person's feature reel." I'm almost certain there's Tumblr-style pictures-with-words-on-them that state precisely that, with a foundation picture of a spool of 35-millimeter film, set to half murkiness. Yet, that does not make me any less inclined to lie wakeful at 3 a.m. thinking about whether I'm not smash hit enough for her.

My DBT therapist used to state, "feelings restart themselves," and instruct me to "get off the wheel" after I had spent a large portion of our session hamstring over something. (What's more, no, Microsoft Word, I'm making an effort not to type "hamstring," so quit policing me with the self-corrector). What I'm attempting to state is that, in evident BPD design, I can belabor on something like this well past the purpose of sanity persuaded it's everything about my inadequacies and not about the way that the creator is in a full-body cast with just an iPhone, a Fentanyl drip, and one working finger.

What's more, in that lies one of the incredible facts of DBT: it's not about you, and you don't have the foggiest idea what occurred. I return by and by to one of my most-utilized aptitudes, Check the Facts. Any individual who's been in an exacting DBT program will relate (and moan) when I state if I were still in treatment, I'd do a conduct investigation of why I sent that second message.

The DBT mindfulness skills frequently want to have bamboo

splinters driven underneath my fingernails, yet this is one of those times when they work. Permit me to survey them and address how they help when managing Facebook-induced paranoia.

States of Mind

If ever there was a period you have to escape Emotion Mind and into Wise Mind, this is it. Regularly, you need to experience Reasonable Mind to arrive. Logic and intellect are your companions about managing Facebook vagueness. For instance, I realize that sending somebody two messages in fourteen days is sufficient. I know she's seen them.

Nonetheless, when I concentrate just on the well-established realities–she hasn't reacted, and she hasn't acknowledged my friend request–I'm ready to see that it's not really about me, similarly as most things on the planet aren't about me. It's particularly not about the way that I'm not enough writer. Individuals have various purposes behind getting things done, or not doing them, by and large. When I'm ready to acknowledge these realities profoundly, I can ease myself into Wise Mind, which I'll realize I've arrived at when the kicking and shouting die down.

"What" Skills (Observe, Describe and Participate)

Observing implies seeing occasions, feelings, and conduct without naming them, ruminating on them, or responding by sticking to pain. I notice that the creator hasn't reacted to me. Nonetheless, I can't watch her feelings or conduct; I can just watch my own. My feelings reveal to me I'm sufficiently bad. They lead to the conduct of keeping awake around evening time stressing, which prompts the conduct of resting later than I'd like the following day, which prompts surliness, which prompts ruminating on the grumpiness, which prompts ruminating regarding why I'm sufficiently bad to be someone's friend. Watching is the initial phase in stopping all that.

Describing is giving a name to what you watch. My DBT therapist used to discuss essential and auxiliary feelings, which I currently talk about with my writing students since they're instrumental when building complex characters. I may think my essential feeling is anger. However, it's genuinely dread. I'm furious somebody would treat me how my Emotion Mind discloses to me I'm being dealt with because I'd never treat somebody that way. After all, I was brought up in Arkansas by a Southern mother, which implies I grew up writing notes to say "thanks" for every little thing. But, the feeling that is driving the anger is fear. Also, what's even more terrifying to somebody with BPD than being overlooked? NOTHING.

Participating is easy to understand, if difficult to do: it implies getting the hellfire off Facebook and going out.

"How" Skills (Non-Judgmentally, One-Mindfully and Effectively):

A non-judgmental stance is monitoring what you've watched and portrayed without judging it. For this situation, I can be furious that the "Seen" notice exists without being angry at the creator. (Truly, what cruel person believed that warning was important? Oh no, judging). When you "weaken your emotions from the realities," as Marsha Linehan says, you can be non-judgmental, which helps push you toward Wise Mind.

One-Mindfully implies remaining present, getting off the wheel, and completely taking care of the things throughout my life to which I have to join in. I might need to play 50 million (alright, five) games of Candy Crush while fanatically checking my approaching messages, however, that won't complete my clothing. I'm certain the genuine individuals in my genuine would welcome it if I wore clean socks and underwear. If I go to the Laundromat, I get the opportunity to smell my Trader Joe's lavender clothing cleanser, and I truly like the smell of that cleanser. Concentrating on the scent of your soap may appear to be a little hippy-dippy, such as something that Twin Peaks specialist with one red and one blue focal point in his glasses would uphold. Yet, it's better than making any valid reason why you won't converse with my messages in your head.

Effectively implies going about as capably as conceivable in the situation you're in, not the situation you need. As such, carry on honestly of socially acceptable behavior, regardless of whether you need to remember what "socially acceptable" signifies. Sending is there any good reason you won't converse with me messages may have been my M.O. Before, yet it's not socially acceptable behavior. If you need to shield somebody from blocking you on Facebook as well as taking out a limiting request, you need to relinquish your annoyance and quit making everything about how you've been insulted.

I may not appreciate utilizing the Core Mindfulness skills; however, I know how to, which is the only thing that is meaningful. What I love about DBT, what I adored about composition out these skills, is that I needed to return and bother them separated because once I utilize one, the others follow.

Chapter 9 - Feeling Regulation Worksheets and Strategies

As people, we will never have full control over what we feel, yet we have much more impact on how we feel than you may have heard.

The skills that allow you to direct and manage your feelings are called 'feeling regulation abilities' (see self-guideline. It doesn't make a pilgrimage to a holy site, or a large number of dollars to gain proficiency with secrets to feeling much improved.

Science-based activities won't just enhance your capacity to understand and control your feelings, yet will also give you the devices to encourage the emotional intelligence of your clients, students, or employees.

The emotion regulation portion focuses on aptitudes that advantage every individual who has feelings (i.e., each human!); however, they are generally gainful for those struggling with mind-set or personality disorders, particularly those with Borderline Personality Disorder (BPD).

In this module, clients figure out how to understand and acknowledge their feelings, lessen their emotional vulnerability and volatility, and reduce emotional suffering.

One of the most significant parts of treatment is perceiving that negative or painful feelings are not inherently bad. Clients are urged to acknowledge that they will, without a doubt, experience negative emotions throughout their life, regardless of how upbeat or even they might be.

Rather than focusing on avoiding or preventing the presence from claiming the negative, DBT clients learn important skills to hold their feelings in check and avoid emotional dysregulation.

What is Emotional Dysregulation?

If emotion regulation is the way toward controlling one's feelings, keeping them in balance and away from limits, at that point, it's most likely simple to make sense of what emotional dysregulation is—the failure to control one's emotional responses.

Emotional dysregulation is a procedure with three fundamental steps:

1. An external or internal event (thinking something sad or experiencing somebody angry) incites a subjective experience (feeling or emotion);

2. A cognitive reaction (thought) is then railed by an emotion-related physiological response (for instance, an expansion in

heart rate or hormonal emission).

3. The procedure culminates in a behavior (avoidance, physical activity, or expression; PCH Treatment Center, n.d.).

Individuals who are struggling with emotional dysregulation respond to generally mild negative occasions in an emotionally exaggerated way. They may cry, scream, charge, fault people around them, or take part in passive-aggressive behaviors or different practices that can disrupt relationships and escalate conflict (PCH Treatment Center, n.d.).

Ongoing research has suggested that emotional dysregulation, particularly when present in those experimenting BPD, is made up of four components:

1. Emotion sensitivity;

2. Heightened and insecure state of mind or feelings;

3. Absence of suitable feeling guideline systems;

4. Plenty of maladaptive feeling guideline systems (Carpenter and Trull, 2013).

DBT Self Help: 3 Emotion Regulation Questionnaires

There are a couple of self-assessment tools available to find out about your emotion regulation abilities. The three generally well known and most evidence-backed scales are incorporated below.

Feeling Guideline Survey

The Emotion Regulation Survey, or ERQ, is the most well-known emotion regulation scale among brain science analysts. It was created in 2003 by James Gross and John Oliver, given five studies spanning the question development, reliability and validity, and structure of the questionnaire.

The scale is made out of 10 things, appraised on a scale from 1 (strongly disagree) to 7 (strongly agree). The scale covers two aspects, the Cognitive Reappraisal feature, the Expressive Suppression aspect, and produces a different score for every aspect.

The six things that make up the Cognitive Reappraisal feature are as per the following:

•	When I need to feel a positive emotion, (such as happiness or delight), I change my thought process;

•	When I need to feel a positive feeling, (such as trouble or outrage), I change my thought process;

•	When I'm threatened with a traumatic situation, I make myself consider it such that helps me stay calm;

•	When I need to feel a positive feeling, I change how I'm thinking about the situation;

•	I control my feelings by changing how I consider the

circumstance I'm in;

•   When I need to feel a positive feeling, I change how I'm thinking about the situation.

The four things that make up the Expressive Suppression feature incorporate;

•   I keep up about my feelings;

•   When I am feeling positive emotions, I am mindful so as not to express them;

•   I control my feelings by not communicating them;

•   When I am feeling negative emotions, I make a point not to expressing them.

Relational Feeling Regulation Questionnaire

The Relational Emotion Regulation Questionnaire, or IERQ, was created to focus on the less attended interpersonal emotion regulation processes, instead of relational procedures. This scale was grown as of late (2016) by scientists Hofmann, Carpenter, and Curtiss.

It consists of 20 things and covers four factors, each containing five items rated on a scale from 1 (not valid for me by any stretch of the imagination) to 5 (extremely true for me).

The four elements and their related things are as per the following:

- **Enhancing Positive Affect:**

  - I like being around others when I'm eager to share my delight;

  - Being within sight of certain others feels great when I'm elated;

  - I like being within sight of others when I feel positive since it magnifies the good feeling;

  - Because happiness is contagious, I search out others when I'm happy;

  - When I feel thrilled, I search out others to satisfy them.

- **Perspective Taking:**

  - It encourages me to manage my depressed state of mind when others bring up that things aren't as bad as they seem;

  - Having people remind me that others are worse causes me when I'm upset;

  - When I am upset, others try to make me feel better by causing me to understand that things could be a lot worse;

- When I am annoyed, others can calm me by advising me not to stress;

- Having individuals telling me not to stress can quiet me down when I am anxious.

- **Soothing:**

  - I search for others to offer me empathy when I'm upset;

  - Feeling regularly upset makes me search out other people who will express sympathy;

  - I seek others for comfort when I feel upset;

  - I look to others when I feel discouraged just to realize that I am loved;

  - When I feel tragic, I search out others for consolation.

- **Social Modeling:**

  - It causes me to feel better to figure out how others managed their feelings;

  - Hearing someone else's thoughts on the most proficient method to deal with things encourages me when I am concerned;

  - Seeing how others would deal with a similar situation helps me when I am frustrated;

- When I'm sad, it causes me to hear how others have managed similar feelings;

- If I'm upset, I like realizing what others would do on the off chance that they were in my circumstance.

Intellectual Feeling Regulation Survey

The 'Intellectual Emotion Regulation Survey', or CERQ, is a scale for recognizing the adapting psychological techniques utilized after a negative experience. It varies from other emotional regulation questionnaires in its attention to the person's thoughts and exclusion of the behavior; it intends to discover what cognitive strategies the individual uses, as opposed to how they carry on.

The scale is made out of 36 things evaluated on a scale from 1 ([almost] never) to 5 ([almost] consistently). It incorporates nine separate cognitive coping strategies, with four things, including every technique.

The nine methodologies and a model thing are incorporated down:

- Self-fault – I feel that I am the person who is responsible for what has occurred;

- Acceptance – I imagine that I need to acknowledge this

has happened;

•	Rumination – I need to understand why I feel how I do about what I have experienced;

•	Positive Refocusing – I consider lovely things that have nothing to do with it;

•	Refocus on Planning – I consider how I can best adapt to the situation;

•	Positive Reappraisal – I believe that I can turn into a stronger person because of what has happened;

•	Putting into Perspective – I imagine that it hasn't been too bad compared with different things;

•	Catastrophizing – I regularly believe that what I have experienced is worse than what others have experienced;

•	Other-fault – I consider the errors others have made in this issue.

DBT Emotion Regulation Strategies and Techniques

Perhaps, the best thing about DBT is its attention to useful, real-world skills and procedures. In this type of treatment, you won't need to stress over unclear thoughts surrounding healing and moving forward; your advisor will have a point by point rundown of skills, procedures, and strategies you can use to begin feeling and improving.

A couple of the best systems and procedures are discussed below.

Understanding and Labeling Feelings

One of the most incredible assets in the feeling guideline is essentially identifying and naming the feelings you are experimenting with.

DBT urges clients to utilize descriptive labels for their emotions, instead of vague or general terms. The thought behind this skill is to deal with a feeling, and you should initially recognize what it is.

Clients of DBT will also find out the difference between primary and secondary feelings, what's more, how to address each in the most supportive manner.

- **Essential feelings:** the initial response to an occasion or triggers in your environment.

- **Auxiliary feelings:** the response to your essential feelings or thoughts.

'Essential feelings' are regularly natural reactions to things around us, such as being tragic when a friend or family member dies, or angry when somebody is rude to us. In any case, auxiliary feelings are more dangerous and more inside our control; we, by and large, have a greater degree of decision about how to react to how we are sad when somebody passes on.

Secondary emotions can push us towards practices that are destructive and maladaptive, making it fundamental to figure out how to acknowledge your essential feeling without deciding for yourself for feeling it.

In DBT meetings, you may talk about legends nearby feelings, such as the possibility that there is a "right" and a "wrong" approach to feeling about specific occasions or circumstances. Our feelings are one of unique, organic experiences that can't be shaped to fit thoughts of what is "typical," and to attempt can be of what is "normal," and to try can be unsafe.

Feelings are adaptive evolutionary traits they created because they helped us work better, both by helping us speak with others and by making us aware of things in our condition that are beneficial or potentially problematic.

Figuring out how to understand, recognize, and label feelings is an enormously helpful skill to have, and not exclusively will it give you a good establishment for dealing with your feelings.

Yet, it will also assist you in understand and empathize with other people.

Letting Go of Painful Emotions

Maybe the most significant emotion regulation skill is figuring out how to give up can be difficult but is worth the effort you invest.

People tend to become stuck when attempting to process negative emotions. Rather than just releasing them, we regularly hold ever tighter to them, fixating on every piece of our emotional experience and asking why it's transpiring.

It sounds inconsistent, yet the demonstration of tolerating that we have feelings we would prefer not to feel can be the way to relinquishing them. When we acknowledge that we are suffering, we prevent running from the difficult feelings and go to face them, and when we do, we may see that it wasn't the huge terrible beast we thought it was, however, it was just a smaller and more manageable beast.

Follow these means to take a shot at your capacity to relinquish negative feelings:

1. Observe your feeling. Recognize that it exists, remain once more from it, and get yourself unstuck from it;

2. Try to experience your feelings as a wave, traveling every which way. You may think that it's helpful to focus on some piece of the emotion, similar to how your body is feeling or some picture about it.

3. Recognize that you are not your feelings. Your feelings are a piece of you. You are more than your feelings;

4. Do not let yourself guide up for the feeling; having it doesn't mean that you need to act. You may simply need to sit that emotion and recognize it. Regularly, acting can intensify and prolong the emotion;

5. Practice LOVING your feelings. This can be a difficult idea. For what reason would we need to love painful emotions?

We can figure out how to love our feelings simply by realizing how to love ourselves (acceptance), and everything else that we can't change our age, our height, spots, the birds that sing early in the morning and wake us up, the climate, the size of our feet, allergies, etc.

Difference Between Healthy and Unhealthy Emotion Regulation Activities

There are numerous methods to assist you in controlling your feelings the right way or to keep up your positive mood and emotional balance. There are also many techniques that, on a superficial level, appear as though they will assist you in keeping your emotional balance; however, upon further thought, reveal themselves to be unhealthy.

Various exercises may work best for you; however, these lists are a good start if you are unsure where to start separating healthy from unhealthy activities.

Healthy activities that assist you in managing your feelings include:

- Talking with friends;

- Exercising;

- Writing in a journal;

- Meditation;

- Therapy;

- Taking care of yourself when physically ill;

- Getting adequate sleep;

- Paying regard for negative thoughts that happen previously or on the other hand after compelling feelings;

- Noticing when you need a break—and taking it!

These exercises are strong since they don't just add better

management of your feelings; they don't cause you any harm.

Unhealthy activities that may appear as though they help, however, hurt, include:

• Abusing alcohol or different substances;

• Self-injury;

• Avoiding or pulling back from troublesome circumstances;

• Physical or verbal animosity;

• Excessive web-based life use, to the avoidance of different responsibilities (Rolston and Lloyd-Richardson, n.d.).

These activities will, in general, make you feel better and help at the time, just as give a superior technique than "total avoidance" of circumstances that you inevitably should face.

When you are engaged to take part in an unhealthy activity, consider an action that builds a sense of achievement instead. Try an activity that will bring about you finding some new information or developing up another expertise, and permit yourself the space to build on it consistently.

Relational Effectiveness

What is the most significant skill an individual can have?

There is a horde of skills that can be added to our collection, upgraded, and improved.

There are many courses, books and articles, countless tips and proposals to improve our lives by developing a certain skill or set of abilities.

But, which one is most important?

There may not be a complete response to that question, yet I think one about the most widely common answers would be: communication (or interpersonal) skills.

It is just a fact that we will experience thousands, even several thousands, of individuals in the course of our life. While we don't have to establish a good impression with every singular we meet (which would be a tough task at any rate), we do need to, in any event, get along with others all around ok to get by.

This is particularly valid for those struggling with a mental disorder like depression, anxiety, or Borderline Personality Disorder (BPD). It tends to be doubly hard for individuals with these obstructions to communicate with others successfully.

Luckily, there are approaches to upgrade your interpersonal effectiveness. Regardless of whether you are a fruitful open speaker or an introverted loner, some assets and activities can improve your relational abilities and your satisfaction.

In case you wish to find out additional information, our Positive Relationships Masterclass© is a finished, science-based training template for specialists and coaches that contains all the materials you'll have to enable your clients to improve their interpersonal skills and relationships, at last upgrading their mental health.

What is the Definition of Interpersonal Effectiveness?

Interpersonal effectiveness, at its generally fundamental, refers to the capacity to interact with others. It includes the skills we use to:

1. Attend to relationships

2. Balance needs versus requests

3. Balance the "needs" and the "should"

4. Build a feeling of authority and self-respect

The objective can break our capacity to associate with others we have as a primary concern for our interactions. There are three main goals to interaction:

1. Gaining our target

2. Maintaining our relationships

3. Keeping our self-respect

Every objective requires interpersonal skills; while some interpersonal skills will be applied, as a rule, a few skills will be particularly significant for achieving one of these objectives.

When we are moving in the direction of picking up our target, we need abilities that include explaining what we need from the association, and distinguishing what we have to do to get the outcomes we need.

While keeping up our relationships is our main goal, we have to see how significant the particular relationship is to us, how we need the individual to feel about us, and what we have to do to keep the relationship going.

At long last, when we will probably keep our self-respect, we will utilize interpersonal skills to assist us in feeling how we might want to feel after the communication is finished and to stick to our qualities and the truth.

Chapter 10 - Relational Effectiveness and Dialectical Behavioral Therapy

Relational adequacy is the main focus of Dialectical Behavioral Therapy (DBT). Indeed, it's the second core skills module in great DBT, with huge amounts of materials and assets committed to improving the client's interpersonal skills.

You may be asking why interpersonal effectiveness is essential to the point that it warrants a whole module in one of the most popular forms of therapy. Without a doubt, communication is significant, yet does it truly require this much time and exertion? Why?

DBT's take is that these aptitudes are so significant because of how we speak with others hugely affects the quality of our relationships with others, and the results of our interactions with others. Like this, the nature of our relationships and the results of our interactions impact our health, our sense of self-esteem and self-confidence, and our extremely understanding of what our identity is.

While there are numerous skills identified with communication and interaction with others, DBT centers around two principle parts:

1. The capacity to request things that you need

2. The capacity to disapprove of requests, when suitable

The Significance of Increasing Your Interpersonal Effectiveness Skills

At this point, you have most likely perceived the significance of having great, or if nothing else, sufficient, communication, and interaction skills. However, you might be feeling that if you have what it takes to speak with others at any rate level of effectiveness, you're set! Why trouble to take a shot at abilities you as of now have?

Like any arrangement of complex abilities, there will never be a point where you have mastered them. Indeed, even the best motivational speakers and advertising specialists are not perfect communicators. There is consistently an opportunity to get better!

Research has given proof that improving these relational abilities prompts constructive results, particularly for clients with Borderline Personality Disorder (BPD). For instance, DBT expertise use has been appeared to improve BPD symptoms overall and the client's relationship capabilities, and also decrease full of feeling insecurity.

6 Games and Activities (for Groups) to Develop Effective Interpersonal Skills

While there are numerous worksheets and individual activities you can participate in to build your interpersonal skills, they are not generally the best method to do this. It's nothing unexpected that the ideal approach to improve your interactions with others is to work on interacting with others!

Not only are group activities commonly more successful in improving interpersonal skills, but they are also regularly more fun. Below, we've recorded and described 5 fun games and exercises that you can practice to improve your interpersonal effectiveness (just as one handout you can use to assess your interpersonal skills).

Skills Assessment Handout

Before trying to improve your interpersonal communication skills, it is a smart thought to discover where you right now are with everyone.

On this page, you will find 29 abilities, such as

- Introducing yourself

- Listening – taking in what individual's state

- Listening – showing interest for individuals

- Responding to laud

- Responding to negative feedback

- Self-exposure as proper

For every expertise, you are told to rate yourself on a scale from 1 to 5, as indicated by the following rubric:

- 1 – I am poor at that expertise

- 2 – I am poor

- 3 – I am now and again great

- 4 – I am typically acceptable

- 5 – I am in every case great

You can take the normal of your evaluations to give yourself a generally speaking "interpersonal effectiveness" skill rating; however, the individual ratings are significant without anyone else.

In case you want to improve your relational abilities, make a point to set up a benchmark first. If you have a gauge to look at the back with, it is a lot simpler to see improvements!

Do whatever it takes not to Listen to Activity

In this fun and possibly educational action, group individuals will get an opportunity to put their acting chops to the test.

The group ought to be broken into sets for this movement. In each pair, one individual ought to be assigned to talk first while the other "listens," before switching roles.

The first speaker, (Partner A), is told to talk for two minutes in a row, about any subject they'd prefer to discuss. While Partner A is speaking, Partner B's main responsibility is to make it clear that the individual isn't tuning in to Partner A by any stretch of the imagination.

Partner B can't utter a word, rather depending on non-verbal communication to share their message to Partner A.

When Partner A's two minutes of talking time are up, Partner B gets two minutes to talk while Partner A "listens."

The gathering will probably find that it is extremely hard to continue talking when their partner is so clearly not tuning in! This is a significant exercise from the movement: that body language assumes a role in communication, and listeners have a huge impact over how the connection goes in addition to those speaking.

When all gathering individuals have gone ahead, both talking and "listening," every individual ought to record their immediate responses to having a speaking partner that is not listening.

They will presumably think of emotions like:

• I felt frustrated.

• I was angry.

• I felt that I wasn't significant.

• I felt like what I was stating must be boring.

• I couldn't continue talking.

• I felt insignificant and unimportant.

Next, group members should take note of the practices that their partner was displaying to show that they weren't tuning in, behaviors like:

• Facing away, with head twisted toward the floor or went to the side

• Avoiding eye to eye connection

• Looking at the floor/roof

• Folded arms/crossed legs

• Blank or bored expression

• Yawning, whistling, scratching or other action

contradictory with active listening

•   Preoccupation (with taking a look at one's surroundings, one's phone, and so on)

•   No collaboration by any means

While this activity is an exaggeration of what it resembles to converse with somebody who isn't listening, this can help the individuals who are not conscious or restricted in their social skills to screen their conduct while interfacing with others.

It's anything but difficult to choose to practice active listening in your interactions. Yet, it's harder to keep the entirety of the objective practices (and the entirety of the decidedly non-target behaviors) as a top priority. Practicing this activity will assist members in identifying and remember the practices that make a person a good listener.

You can discover this activity of the handout mentioned above (Interpersonal Skills Exercises).

Sabotage Exercise

This is another great exercise that incorporates poor interpersonal behaviors to make you understand how it works.

This activity ought to be undertaken in a genuinely large group sufficiently huge to break into a few groups of four to five individuals in any event.

Educate each group to take around 10 minutes to brainstorm, discuss, and list all the manners they can consider to sabotage a group assignment. Anything they can consider is fair game–it simply should be something disruptive enough to drive a group task directly out of control!

When each group has a good-sized list of approaches to sabotage a group assignment, gather into the bigger group again and think about responses. Keep in touch with them all on the chalkboard, whiteboard, or a flip board in the front of the room.

Next, change the groups and teach them to create a 5-to 10-point contract with settled upon rules for successful group work. Gathering individuals should draw from the sabotage ideas (i.e., what not to accomplish for successful group work) to identify smart thoughts (i.e., what to do for successful group work).

For instance, if a group listed "don't speak with any of the other group members" as an approach to sabotage the group assignment, they may think of something like "speak with other gathering individuals regularly" as a rule for effective gathering work.

This activity will enable members to realize what makes for a positive gathering experience, while also allowing them to have a positive gathering experience along the way.

Gathering Strengths and Weaknesses

Groups have one important advantage over individuals with regards to achieving work–they can offset individuals' weaknesses, complement their qualities, and carry a balance to the group.

Group members will take part in some critical thinking and discussion about their strengths and weaknesses in this activity, just as the strengths and weaknesses of the other gathering individuals and the group as a whole.

To check out this activity, train the group to consider the strengths and weaknesses of every individual group member. Urge them to be honest, however kind to each other, particularly while talking about weaknesses.

When each group has thought of a good list of strengths and weaknesses for each gathering part, have each gathering consider how these will affect group dynamics. What qualities will positively influence group interactions? Which weaknesses can mess up group interactions?

At last, have each group examine the synthesis of a "great" group. Is it better to have individuals with similar characteristics or a wide range of personalities, capacities, and aptitudes?

This discussion will assist members to think critically about what makes a decent group, how various personalities interact, and how to change your behavior, group norms, or desires to coordinate the varying personalities and abilities of others.

This activity is also described on page 14 of the gift on interpersonal skills (Interpersonal Skills Exercises).

Count the Squares

This game is a fun and connecting approach to support group interaction and communication.

All you need is this picture (or similar picture of different squares), showed on a PowerPoint introduction or the divider or board at the front of the room.

In the initial step, give the gathering a few minutes to independently include the number of squares in the figure and record their answer. They ought to do this without speaking to others.

Next, have each gathering part get out the number of squares they checked. Write these down on the board.

Presently educate every member to discover somebody to match up with and count the squares once more. They can converse with one another while determining what number of squares there are.

At long last, have the participants form groups of four to five individuals each and teach them to check the squares once again. When they have completed, by and by bringing down the numbers, each group counted.

At least one group will very certainly have tallied the right number of squares, which is 40. Have this gathering walk the remainder of the members through how they got to 40.

At long last, lead the whole group through a conversation of group synergy, and why the checks (likely) kept getting closer and closer to 40 as more individuals got together to take care of the issue.

Members will find out about the importance of good group communication, practice working two by two and in gatherings, and ideally have a great time finishing this action.

Non-Verbal Introduction Game

This game is a pleasant bend on an old exemplary–meeting a renewed individual and introducing them with the group.

You should design this game on the main day of group therapy, training, or another movement to make the most of the chance to present each gathering part.

Have the group members pair up with an individual sitting close to them. Instruct them to acquaint themselves with one another and include something interesting or unusual about themselves.

When each pair has been presented and has discovered something interesting about the other individual, take the focus back to the larger group.

Tell the group members that every individual must introduce their partner with the gathering, yet with a catch—they can't utilize words or props! Each partner must present the other partner with activities as they were.

This game isn't just a great icebreaker for introducing individuals with each other; it's also a great path for group members to see both the utility of verbal communication (something you may perceive when you can't utilize it!) and the significance of non-verbal correspondence.

In case you have time, you can lead the gathering in a conversation of non-verbal communication, the signs we get on in other people groups' behavior, and how getting feedback from those you are communicating with is essential.

3 Ways to Advance Your Relational Effectiveness in the Workplace

However, there are numerous approaches to chip away at your interpersonal skills, and it is somewhat harder to discover techniques for improving your work-specific interpersonal effectiveness.

Fortunately, the greater part of these abilities transfers nicely from treatment to family life, communications with companions, and the work environment. Also, there are a few activities and assets created to improve work-related interpersonal skills directly.

Beneath, you will find a couple of various approaches to improve your communication at work.

Relational Effectiveness Skills Handout

This helpful handout can be checked on and come back to while you or your client are working on enhancing interpersonal effectiveness.

It diagrams the skills expected to communicate effectively with others, isolated into three various ranges of abilities:

- Objective Effectiveness

- Relationship Effectiveness

- Self-Respect Effectiveness

For each set, there is a convenient abbreviation to assist you in recollecting which abilities are included.

For objective effectiveness, the acronym is "Beloved MAN," and the abilities are:

- D – Describe: utilize clear and concrete terms to portray what you need.

- E – Express: let others realize how a circumstance causes you to feel by clearly expressing your emotions; don't expect others should guess what you might be thinking.

- A – Assert: don't steer clear of the real issue—state what you have to state.

- R – Reinforce: reward individuals who react well, and strengthen why your ideal result is sure.

- M – Mindful: remember the target of the association; it tends to be anything but difficult to get diverted unsafe contentions and lose center.

- A – Appear: seem certain; think about your stance, tone, eye to eye connection, and non-verbal communication.

- N – Negotiate: nobody can have all that they ask for from

cooperation constantly; be available to an arrangement.

These skills allow the individuals who practice them too viably and express their needs and wants and get what they look for from an association.

The abbreviation for relationship adequacy is "GIVE":

•   G – Gentle: don't attack, undermine, or express judgment during your collaborations; acknowledge the occasional "no" for your requests.

•   I – Interested: show enthusiasm by tuning in to the next individual without interfering.

•   V – Validate: be outwardly approving to the next individual's musings and emotions; recognize their feelings, perceive when your requests are requesting, and regard their feelings.

•   E – Easy: have a simple mentality; attempt to smile and act happy.

These aptitudes help individuals to keep up relationships with others through fostering positive interactions.

At last, the abbreviation for a sense of self-respect effectiveness is "Quick":

•   F – Fair: be reasonable, not exclusively to other people yet also to yourself.

- A – Apologies: don't apologize except if it's justified; don't apologize for making a request, having an opinion, or disagreeing.

- S – Stick to Values: don't bargain your qualities just to be preferred or to get what you need; go to bat for what you have faith in.

- T – Truthful: avoid dishonesty, such as distortion, acting helplessly as a type of control, or by and large lying.

The self-respect skill set, will help shield you from selling your qualities and beliefs to get approval or get what you need.

Realizing what these skills are and how they can be applied is the initial move towards improving your capacity to connect with others. You can discover this gift online at this link.

Radical Acceptance Worksheet

This worksheet causes you to identify and understand a circumstance you are trying to acknowledge, regardless of whether it is at work, in your own life, with your family, or something completely different. Whatever troublesome thing you are working through, you can utilize this worksheet to assist yourself in accepting the truth of your circumstance.

To start with, the worksheet teaches you to respond to the

inquiry, "What is the issue or circumstance?"

Next, you will describe the piece of this circumstance that is hard for you to acknowledge.

At that point, you describe the truth of that circumstance. Think critically about the truth; don't simply record in one word the description of the circumstance to be, you can write what you feel typing, even the worst interpretation of the circumstance is.

In the wake of describing the truth, consider the causes that drove up that reality (clue: you will receive most likely notice that a large number of them are outside of your control!).

Next, you practice acknowledgment with the entire self (brain, body, and soul) and describe how you did this. The worksheet urges you to try the following:

"Inhale deeply, put your body into an open, accepting posture, and notice and let go of thoughts and emotions that battle the truth. Practice skills for acceptance, such as half-grin, awareness exercises, or petition. Concentrate on a statement of acceptance, such as "what will be will be" or "everything is as it ought to be."

At long last, you rate your distress tolerance about this difficult situation both when rehearsing radical acceptance, on a scale from 0 (you can't take it) to 100 (all out an acknowledgment of the real world).

Compass Points Emotional Intelligence Activity

This activity from the National School Reform Faculty is a fantastic way for a group to improve their emotional intelligence together.

To get ready for this activity, make four signs—North, South, East, and West—and post them on the room walls. Under each point, work out the qualities related to each sign:

- North: Acting

  o Likes to act, try things, make a plunge; "How about we do it!"

- East: Speculating

  o Likes to take a look at the 10,000-foot view and all the potential outcomes before acting.

- South: Caring

To start the action, call attention to the four focuses on the members and request that they read everyone, selecting the one that most accurately captures how they work with others on groups. Have them stride over to that point and stay there for the movement.

When every member has picked a compass point, request that

they review an individual past group experience that was extremely positive or exceptionally negative. They shouldn't share this experience still. However, they should remember it to talk about later.

Then, have the natural groups (framed by compass point selection) designate three situations among themselves:

- Recorder – record the reactions of the gathering

- Timekeeper – keep the gathering individuals on the task

- Spokesperson – share out for the benefit of the gathering when time is up

When the jobs have been allotted, give 5 to 8 minutes to the groups to react to the following questions:

1. What are the strengths of your style?

2. What are the limitations of your style?

3. What style do you find generally hard to work with, and why?

4. What do individuals from other "bearings" or styles need to think about you so you can cooperate effectively?

5. What's one thing you esteem about every one of the other three styles?

When each group has examined these five questions and

thought of something to impart to the bigger gathering, have them share their reactions. You may hear things like:

•	North gets on edge with West's requirement for subtleties.

•	West gets disappointed by North's inclination to act previously arranging.

•	South group individuals want personal connections and get awkward when colleagues' emotional needs aren't met.

•	East group individuals get bored when West gets mired in details; East gets disappointed when North makes a plunge before concurring on enormous objectives.

When members have shared their responses to the five questions, request that they review their extremely positive or negative team experience. Advise them to pause for a minute or two to think about whether there was anything they gained from this activity that causes them to all the more likely understand why their positive group experience was certain, or why their negative group experience was negative. This can be an extraordinary method to provoke some "a-ha!" minutes.

At last, move to the finish of the activity and give members a couple of minutes to share their key takeaways from the activity. Some groups will feature various takeaways; however, make a point to point these out if no one brings them up:

•   This action builds our awareness with our own and others' preferences.

•   Increased awareness makes way for sympathy.

•   Our preferences have their strengths and limitations.

•   A decent variety of preferences is the thing that makes for better teamwork and results.

You can discover more data on this activity here.

A Take Home Message

In this piece, we characterized interpersonal effectiveness, described its significance as far as Dialectical Behavioral Therapy, and gave a few different ways to you or your clients to take a shot at improving interpersonal skills.

Chapter 11 - Oversee Emotions and Reduce Stress with DBT

DBT is useful for individuals who struggle to deal with their emotions (e.g., fast mindset changes, intense and debilitating feelings, and so on). The larger objective is to acquire "a life worth living" by figuring out how to endure trouble and improve relationships.

DBT has been demonstrated to be viable in reducing suicidal behaviors, hospitalizations, and issues with anger, depression, and sadness. The key issue that DBT treats is emotion dysregulation, characterized as a combination of extreme emotional vulnerability with trouble in controlling feelings once they are aroused.

Through DBT, you will become familiar with a variety of skills to deal with your feelings, the impulsive, and almost automatic behaviors that regularly go with strong feelings. You will chip away at a highly personalized plan to decrease the behaviors getting the way of your objectives and to expand your utilization of skillful behaviors.

Oversee Emotions, Tolerate Stress and Avoid Risky Behavior

The Four Stages of DBT are:

Stage I: DBT works to treat side effects and build skills in four specific areas:

1. **Emotion Regulation**: Learning some abilities to manage huge feelings like anger, blame, disgrace, misery, or anxiety. Figuring out how not to be overwhelmed by those emotions. The most effective method to experience a greater amount of the feelings you need. The most effective method to change feelings you don't need. Instructions to reduce the power of specific feelings. The most effective method to understand the motivation behind feelings.

2. **Distress Tolerance**: Learning some abilities to manage difficult times or get past the night when things are really bad, without falling back on unwanted or risky behaviors. Learning approaches to acknowledge life, all things considered, in any event, when you don't care for specific pieces of it. Being all the more accepting of yourself.

3. **Interpersonal Effectiveness:** Learning skills to state "no" without feeling guilty. Figuring out how to feel OK about requesting what you need. Setting limits and saying "no"

without feeling you'll upset anybody. Dealing with relationship difficulties without cutting off the association. Correctly saying the correct thing at the right time.

4. **Mindfulness:** Learning how to live at the time. Figuring out how to control your mind without it controlling you. The most effective method to do each thing in turn. The most effective method to experience life with its high points and low points without fleeing from it. Step by step instructions to see the world how it truly is with your eyes open. Instructions to take part in your own life, to be non-critical of yourself as well as other people, and to get what you need in the best way.

Stage II: DBT addresses your inhibited emotional experiences

Before moving to Stage II, it is expected that your behavior is presently leveled out, yet you are suffering "peacefully." The objective of Stage II is to assist you in moving from a condition of quiet desperation to one of full emotional experiencing. This is the phase wherein post-traumatic stress disorder (PTSD) would be dealt with.

Stage III: DBT centers on issues in living

The objective of this stage is that the client has a life of ordinary happiness and unhappiness.

Stage IV: DBT centers on moving from incompleteness to completeness

This stage regularly starts once treatment is finished with people proceeding to investigate their life way.

It is difficult to eliminate stress from our lives. Also, there are no simple or all universal responses to battle the issues of willpower and fatigue that interfere with making life changes. Next are a few procedures instructed in DBT that many have found helpful in reducing painful and debilitating emotions.

Perceive how you manage stress. Emotion regulation skills incorporate figuring out how to identify and label current feelings. In DBT, you figure out how to watch the provoking occasion, thoughts, body sensations, activity desires, and actual actions related to pressure. Recognizing and understanding your very own understanding of pressure can assist you in bettering react when you are stressed.

Change each behavior at a time. DBT emphasizes doing things that cause you to feel capable, self-assured, in charge, and able. These can be little achievements that you do each day or steps towards large accomplishments. To remain centered, DBT shows Mindfulness aptitudes. When you're focused and overwhelmed, it's anything but difficult to get dissipated and distracted by numerous stressors and tasks.

Deal with yourself. Once in a while, it's important to focus on accepting the present circumstance and find ways to survive and tolerate the second without engaging in unhealthy behaviors that bring even more issues. Ameliorating, sustaining, and being gentle and kind to yourself is fundamental when you're focused.

Request support. Over a portion of the women surveyed reported spending time with friends as a technique to manage stress. Relationships and associating with others is a key stress management strategy for ladies. In any case, support is something beyond associating with others. It's also about getting what you need to deal with your life more readily. As per the pressure overview, "Six fold the number of ladies as men state that having more assistance with family unit tasks would permit them to improve their resolution." DBT abilities organize getting transforms you need and need and keeping up associations with the individuals throughout your life while keeping up your confidence. These are basic skills for ladies, who are frequently dealing with different, competing demands.

Why DBT works where different therapies fail

Brenda, a lady in her late thirties, had extreme tension that hadn't shown signs of improvement through past treatments. She would have alarm attacks on the train that occasionally kept her from getting to her appointments. She would detach, not reaching out to friends since she was afraid they might not have any desire to hear from her. Brenda also found that her connections tended as rough. At that point, she would break up with her partner, content him non-stop the next, begging him to reunite.

Seeing that the then-current treatment was not working, Brenda's advisor referred her for more intensive treatment, which I've as often as possible had success with. As an advisor, it's regular for me to meet individuals who have tried therapy many times before, now and again, without effective goals of the issues, they're looking for help. I practice a sort of psychotherapy that regularly works where different methods of treatment therapy have failed: Dialectical Behavior Therapy (DBT). Much of the time, DBT has offered my clients a great success. Things being what they are, what is DBT, how can it work, and for what reason does it succeed where other treatment techniques do not?

DBT Fills in the Holes Left by Fixed CBT

Rationalistic Behavior Therapy was initially evolved by clinician Dr. Marsha Linehan in her work with ladies who had been hospitalized in the wake of endeavoring self-destruction or genuine self-hurt. As well-being proficient who thinks deeply about the contribution to her patient's effective treatments, Dr. Linehan, at first, practiced Cognitive Behavioral Therapy (CBT), a kind of treatment that promotes changing thoughts, feelings, and practices to manage and decrease anxiety.

CBT is regularly viewed as the highest quality level in anxiety treatments. In any case, Dr. Linehan found that standard CBT wasn't working with her clients. CBT's emphasis on changing thoughts and behaviors didn't do what's necessary to help her clients accept where they are. The CBT procedures alone were too invalidating to consider peopling, who regularly found concepts, such as cognitive distortions to infer that their thoughts and emotions weren't right. Dr. Linehan found that something other than what's expected was required - a technique that recognizes and supports reality after that clients' experiences are based.

This is the place DBT comes in: Dialectical Behavior Therapy is a kind of Cognitive Behavioral Therapy; however, what makes it one of a kind is its emphasis on mindfulness dialectical thinking. Instead of just regarding side effects as issues to be tackled, DBT places similarly significant importance on the acknowledgment of encounters as they are at this time. It is one of a few acknowledgment based behavior treatments (ABBTs).

How Dialectical Thinking Plays a Crucial Role in Treatment

DBT centers around dialectical thinking: dialectics refers to a philosophical position where two thoughts or truths, apparently restricted to each other, can exist simultaneously. For instance, an individual coming to treatment may require both acceptance of where they are at present, just as inspiration to change. As such, they have to perceive that everything is actually as it ought to be, and simultaneously realize that they should improve and try harder to create positive change.

How Does DBT Help with Anxiety?

Feelings serve significant functions in our lives. Essential feelings linked to anxiety, such as dread, can now and again bode well—when there is a risk to our life, health, or well-being, fear can motivate us to act and ensure ourselves. On occasion, be that as it may, feelings like fear emerge when they are not useful or gainful. These feelings can be hard to adapt to and manage, leading to anxiety and distress.

DBT works through the way toward learning emotional and cognitive skills (acquisition), and in this way, applying those abilities to your life (generalization). By and large, DBT tackles difficult and distressing emotions. It can assist you in improving your ability for emotional regulation, that is, your capacity to control the feelings you have.

Getting ready Mindfulness and Distress Tolerance Skills with DBT

Through the DBT aptitudes preparing to gather, clients learn abilities, such as care and distress tolerance techniques that guide in having the option to accept the present moment with willingness, as opposed to fighting reality. These methods could incorporate breathing exercises, counting to ten, or holding an ice cube to carry mindfulness and acceptance to the present. Activities like this urge us to decide to acknowledge what's going on at the time.

DBT's emotion regulation skills incorporate watching and depicting feelings, alongside a systematic toolkit for altering emotions you need to change. These devices incorporate checking the facts of a situation, acting opposite to the activity desire of the feeling, and critical thinking to change the occasion prompting a specific emotional reaction.

Changing and influencing feelings is a central goal of DBT; however, before you can get to this progression, it is basic to understand where these feelings are originating from and why they emerge. The "understanding and recognizing" venture of

DBT is one of the primary features that separates it from regular CBT. This methodology supports the careful and non-judgmental observation and description of emotional experiences. The expansion of this perspective makes DBT powerful over a range of mental health problems, including anxiety disorders, because the abilities you take in assist you in separating feelings from facts, allowing you to work with and manage emotions effectively.

Utilizing DBT to Develop Emotional Skills and Alleviate Anxiety

Far-reaching DBT comprises of several parts, including individual therapy with a trained therapist, group skills training, individual skills training (regularly available by phone), and the therapist's participation in a consultation group. All of these parts cooperate to guarantee that DBT offers abilities you can try to cause you to feel more in charge and accountable for how you feel and how you live in your environmental factors. In case you are living with a nervousness issue, you likely realize that feeling responsible for yourself is a very significant validating feeling.

For Brenda's situation, feeling guideline abilities, such as Opposite Action helped her methodology, rather than avoid situations where she felt fearful. Care abilities helped her accept the current second, and she had the option to carry more happiness and importance to her life through healthy relationships.

Dialectical Behavior Therapy (DBT) for PTSD

Dialectical behavior therapy (DBT) was initially evolved to help people struggling with the symptoms of borderline personality disorder (BPD).

Numerous individuals with BPD also have PTSD and bad habit versa. Although people with PTSD and BPD have various symptoms, they share a portion of similar issues, such as

- Difficulty managing emotions

- Interpersonal issues

- High risk of impulsive behavior

You won't be surprised at that point, to find that a few scientists are beginning to explore whether DBT may help individuals with PTSD.

Investigating the Usefulness of DBT for PTSD

The skills utilized in DBT, initially developed for individuals with BPD, may also greatly benefit people with PTSD.

Much the same as people with BPD, people with PTSD have issues dealing with their emotions. They may also have issues with connections or take part in destructive behaviors, such as deliberate self-harm.

To investigate whether DBT may be effective in individuals with PTSD, a gathering of scientists at the Dominant Institute of Mental Health in Mannheim, Germany, rewarded a gathering of ladies who had PTSD (from youth sexual abuse) using an intensive treatment that joined DBT and traditional CBT ways to deal with PTSD treatment, such as presentation. The joint treatment was referred to as DBT-PTSD.

Following three months of treatment, the analysts found that DBT-PTSD fundamentally reduced the women's PTSD symptoms, including depression and anxiety. And, the ladies' PTSD symptoms were all the while improving a month and a half after they finished the treatment, suggesting that they may have learned skills during the study that helped them keep on recover from PTSD after the treatment ended.

Chapter 12 - Persuasive Behavior Therapy for Eating Disorders

There are numerous choices when choosing which kind of treatment to look for an eating disorder. One type of therapy you may be offered is dialectical behavior therapy (DBT).

DBT is a particular kind of cognitive-behavioral treatment. It was shaped in the late 1970s by Marsha Linehan, Ph.D. to treat chronically suicidal people determined to have a borderline personality disorder (BPD). It is currently recognized as the treatment of decision for this population. Also, researches have demonstrated it is powerful for a scope of other mental issues counting substance reliance, misery, post-traumatic stress disorder (PTSD), and dietary issues.

"Dialectical" means that in DBT, specialists and clients endeavor to offset change with acknowledgment, two seemingly opposing forces, or strategies. For instance, while undergoing dialectical behavior therapy, your advisor will work with you to both acknowledge yourself as you may be, and are also roused to change.

DBT Requires Five Components

Full follower DBT treatment requires five components:

1. DBT Skills Training

DBT skills training ordinarily happens in a group format run like a class during which group leaders teach behavioral skills and assign schoolwork. The schoolwork assists clients in working on utilizing the abilities in their everyday lives. Groups meet on a week after week basis, and it takes 24 weeks to get through the full skills curriculum.

Abilities training comprises of four modules:

- **Mindfulness:** the act of being fully aware and present at the time

- **Distress Tolerance:** how to tolerate distressing feelings

- **Interpersonal Effectiveness**: how to communicate one's needs and defined limits to build healthy relationships

- **Emotion Regulation**: how to change feelings that you need to change

2. Singular Therapy

DBT singular therapy focuses on increasing client motivation and helping clients to apply the skills to challenges and events in their lives. As a rule, singular therapy happens once every week for whatever length of time the client is getting help, and it runs all the while with DBT skills training.

3. Training to Ensure Generalization of Skills

DBT utilizes phone training to give in-the-second help. The objective is to coach clients on the most proficient method to utilize their DBT skills to effectively adapt to difficult circumstances that emerge in their everyday lives. Clients can call their therapist between meetings to get training at the times when they need help.

4. Structure of the Environment with Case Management

Case management strategies help the client figure out how to deal with their own life, such as their physical and social environments.

5. DBT Consultation Team to Support the Therapist

The DBT consultation team provides basic help to the different team members who give the different parts of the DBT treatment, including singular advisors, skills training group leaders, case managers, and other people who help treat the client or patient.

Different Types of DBT

There are numerous advisors who use DBT abilities in singular treatment with clients. A few therapists also may offer a standalone DBT skills-training group. However, any of these segments alone are false or completely adherent DBT treatment. These individual components of DBT treatment may, at present, be useful yet may not be as getting each of the five components of the treatment. Dialectical behavior therapy has also been adjusted for use in private and inpatient behavior settings.

Does Dialectical Behavior Therapy (DBT) Work for Eating Disorders?

Although CBT has demonstrated viable for some patients with eating disorders and is normally suggested as the first line of treatment, it doesn't work for everybody. This has led researchers to search for different medicines that may work for patients who don't react to CBT. Specialists in eating disorders who found out about DBT drew a relationship between the capacity of an eating disorder, behaviors in eating disorder patients, and the capacity of self-injury in borderline personality disorder patients. The two kinds of practices will, in general, give temporary relief from negative feelings. In this manner, showing patients how to control and oversee impact bodes well.

The outcomes have been promising as the treatment appears successful in easing back or stopping problematic behaviors in eating issues. Regardless, a huge part of the examination that has been done hasn't compared dialectical behavior therapy with different medicines (or to no treatment by any means).

The one study that compared DBT with active comparison group therapy for binge eating food found no real differences; the two medicines worked similarly well.

The vast majority of the investigations directed on dialectical behavior therapy took a look at rewarding individuals with overeating confusion and bulimia nervosa, not anorexia nervosa.

Who Should Try Dialectical Behavior Therapy?

Given the flow explore into on dialectical behavior therapy and eating problems, it is probably going to be generally useful for individuals experiencing bulimia nervosa or binge eating disorder. It is also likely to be useful for clients who are experiencing borderline personality disorder as well as serious feelings; however, it is an eating problem. DBT is regularly more intensive, more costly, and longer-term than individual outpatient treatment, such as CBT, as isn't normally utilized as a first-line treatment. It might be an amazing choice for patients who have not made upgrades with CBT or other individual psychotherapies, and who battle with gorge consuming food scenes activated by negative feelings.

Diagnosing Histrionic Personality

Histrionic personality disorder (HPD) first showed up in the Diagnostic and Statistical Manual of Mental Disorders (DSM) in 1980. It is named a Cluster B personality disorder, which means it includes impulsivity and emotionality. Since HPD's consideration in the DSM, psychological wellness experts have contended whether it ought to be viewed as its diagnosis.

With a prevalence rate of just 1.8%, HPD is minimal regular of the Cluster B personality disorders. It frequently co-occurs with narcissistic personality (NPD) and borderline personality (BPD). Given this specific situation, a few specialists trust that HPD ought to be delegated a subtype of narcissism or borderline personality.

Others contend that the symptoms of histrionic personality are distinct enough to warrant their diagnosis. The latest release of the (DSM-5) despite everything records HPD as a separate condition.

Why is getting the right diagnosis important?

By and large, individuals with histrionic personality can work at a high level. They may experience trouble recognizing their symptoms as a mental health concern, in any event, when said symptoms cause trouble. This can make determination and treatment difficult.

Suppositions about the significance of diagnosis differ. Some professionals believe diagnosing a particular condition is less necessary than addressing a person's distress. Other professionals who accept a diagnosis helps them build up clear objectives for therapy. At times, accepting a diagnosis of histrionic personality may enable an individual to comprehend their side effects all the more unmistakably?

Having a good comprehension of one's side effects can be essential to effective therapy. The distress brought about by HPD can lead to co-occurring mental health issues. For instance, an individual may look for help for depressive symptoms brought about by HPD. If the base of the depression (the HPD) isn't tended to, at that point, treatment might be less effective.

Misdiagnosis can also hurt. Treatment designed to improve the symptoms of one condition may not be as effective for another. For instance, an individual with HPD may benefit from cognitive-behavioral therapy (CBT), which can assist individuals in addressing negative thoughts. But CBT would be substantially less powerful for somebody with BPD. Specialists think about dialectical behavior therapy, which strongly emphasizes feelings and social work, the best treatment for BPD.

Histrionic personality vs. borderline personality

Borderline personality (BPD) is another group B personality disorder. HPD and BPD share a few characteristics, and it's possible to have the two conditions. But, they are, actually, various diagnoses.

Like histrionic personality, BPD may include impulsive and attention-seeking behavior. However, existing research doesn't suggest people with BPD effectively want to be the center of attention. Or maybe, their activities are frequently motivated by fear of surrender. They are also bound to engage in self-destructive behavior than those with HPD.

An example of unstable relationships can be seen with both diagnoses. An individual with a histrionic personality may experience difficulty keeping up a relationship because of their coy conduct. They may leave a drawn relationship out of fatigue. In the meantime, somebody with BPD may feel rage at the minor thought of a relationship falling apart. This anger can turn into a self-fulfilling prophecy and drive their partner away.

Finally, both diagnoses include quickly changing emotions. However, those with histrionic personalities are bound to communicate in a "theatrical" way. They are more reluctant to report the feelings of deep emptiness, which are basic in marginal character.

How does the histrionic personality differ from vanity?

Narcissism, or narcissistic disorder issue (NPD), is an additional group B personality disorder. It's like HPD from multiple points of view. However, there are a couple of key contrasts.

One symptomatic need for narcissism is an absence of sympathy. Individuals with this condition may ignore how others feel and have little compassion. Individuals with histrionic personality may take part in self-centered behavior, but they don't necessarily lack empathy.

Another significant distinction lies in the explanations behind attention-seeking behavior. Individuals with narcissism need to be recognized as unique as or better than others. They frequently lie or exaggerate their achievements to receive praise, acknowledgment, or status. Individuals with HPD need the attention of others yet may think less about how they get it. They may assume the role of victimhood and allow others to consider them as fragile or helpless.

Histrionic personality or typical teenage behavior?

Young people will, in general, experience intense feelings and respond in manners that may appear to be extreme to friends and family. They may also appear to be self-centered, suggestible, and impulsive, other huge characteristics of HPD. Since histrionic personality symptoms frequently show up during the teenage years, they might be mistaken with ordinary adolescent experiences. This can make diagnosing HPD difficult.

Frequently the way to determining whether a teen has histrionic personality is to look at the setting of their behaviors. Have the symptoms gone on for in any event a year? Does the individual show unusual behavior constantly, or exactly when they are in a bad mood? Could the teen be consuming any drugs (recreational or prescribed) that may influence their feelings?

Personality is unique and comprised of numerous elements. Somebody can look for attention, carry on drastically, or experience extreme feelings without having HPD. What makes HPD an emotional wellness determination is the pain and trouble it causes in the day-by-day life. An individual with a histrionic personality may regret alienating others or acting impulsively, yet feel unable to change.

Chapter 13 - How You Can Overcome Intrusive Thoughts

Have you at any point needed to avoid thinking of a specific experience or subject just to find that it persistently encroaches into your contemplations and exercises? Also, the more you attempt to suppress the idea, the more interfering it becomes? Wegner, a Harvard University Professor, terms these musings "white bears" and, in the wake of experiencing these thoughts 25 years prior, dug into examine on thought suppression.

Through 10 years of research, he found that when we do whatever it takes not to consider something part of the mind keeps away from the idea, yet another part "checks in" to ensure the idea isn't coming up. Ironically, this "checking in" to ensure the idea isn't coming up, brings it to mind.

So what do you do when your brain inevitably "checks in" with those thoughts you most need to keep out of your awareness? In an introduction for the American Psychological Association, Wegner depicted a few methodologies to smother thoughts that barge in any event, when you are making an effort not to think them.

The strategies he defined include:

- Choose an absorbing disruption and focus on that. Try to locate an interesting movement to divert your attention, such as puzzles, emotional movies, and engaging discussion, or a favorite hobby.

- Try to delay the idea. As per Wegner, some examination recommends that putting aside thirty minutes to stress at a specific time during the day can decrease stress and intrusive thoughts the rest of the day.

- Cut back on performing multiple tasks. In another examination, people under expanded mental burden (say from trying to finish numerous assignments without a moment's delay) show an expansion in thoughts of death, which are a typical intrusive and unwanted thought for many.

- Expose yourself to the idea. Allowing yourself to consider unwanted subjects in controlled manners can decrease the probability that they will spring up and intrude into your thoughts at unwanted times.

- Meditation and mindfulness. In mindfulness exercises, you work on focusing attention, noticing distractions, such as intrusive thoughts and refocusing. Like with a game, practice improves your skill level. After some time, you can prepare your psyche to see diverting thoughts and rapidly refocus.

Instructions to Incorporate Into Pain Management

There is a lot of proof to help the viability of different cognitive-behavioral interventions for reducing pain force and improving a patient's coping skills. Behavioral medicine approaches mean to modify the general pain experience, help reestablish working, and improve the personal satisfaction of patients who suffer from chronic pain. The widest interventions include acceptance and commitment therapy (ACT) and traditional cognitive-behavioral therapy (CBT).

The writing has indicated that ACT compares well and traditional CBT in the treatment of chronic pain among various populations, incorporating cancer patients, people in a university-based pain management outpatient clinic, Australian patients at a pain management unit, and network tests, including a little representation of veterans. The investigation has also established that for chronic pain, both ACT and CBT mediations decrease pain intensity, disability, and pain interference.

Moreover, both ACT and CBT interventions have been found to expand status to receive a self-management approach and make changes in how an individual copes with chronic pain. However, considerable variability in results exists between these interventions: ACT and CBT don't have uniform impacts and are not viable for all patients. For instance, ACT and traditional CBT will, in general, cover as far as social procedures and systems, yet there are explicit theoretical differences that exist as to the role of cognition and emotional regulation strategies.

Acknowledgment and Assurance Therapy

Continuing pain is an intricate biopsychosocial situation, requiring a multimodal way to deal with management. In light of behavior theory, the principal wave of behavioral medicine interventions commenced during the 1920s, while the subsequent wave, in light of cognitive-behavioral theory, emerged during the 1970s. ACT is one of the more effectively looked into approaches among the third aware of developing psychotherapies.

ACT is particular from different mindfulness-based interventions, such as mindfulness-based stress reduction (MBSR), mindfulness-based cognitive therapy (MBCT), and dialectical behavior therapy (DBT). For instance, MBSR utilizes a combination of mindfulness meditation, body mindfulness, and yoga to assist individuals in getting more careful. MBCT utilizes traditional CBT strategies and includes care meditation. Care is a core exercise utilized in DBT, which combines standard subjective behavior strategies for feeling guidelines with ideas of misery resistance got from Buddhist reflective practice. What separates ACT is that it is a type of clinical behavioral technique that utilizes acknowledgment and care techniques, blended in with responsibility and behavior-change strategies, to increase psychological flexibility.

ACT is a style of treatment with a great deal of flexibility, and the remedial procedure is more experiential than academic. Consequently, efficacy will rely to a great extent upon the patient's level of commitment and participation in treatment. The experiential components experiment for patients to teach and exercise new and more flexible ways of reacting to pain. The simple idea of ACT is for patients to move their primary focus from decreasing or eliminating pain to completely engaging in their lives. ACT is tied in with changing how patients relate with their internal experiences; it is about living better.

An essential goal of treatment is for the patient to suffer less by getting effectively associated with what they truly care about and what makes a difference most in their lives, despite having and suffering from pain. ACT cure is problematic, as there are no modest answers for chronic pain. Patients may feel a scope of feelings (angry, sad, on edge, or uncomfortable) during the intervention; however, this reaction is natural and entirely normal. The job of the specialist is to assist patients in accepting whatever discomfort exists, both physical and emotional, while proceeding to live their lives as per their values. Doing so can assist patients in rolling out important improvements in their lives and reduce suffering.

Various established protocols have been published for ACT for chronic pain. One protocol proposed a 4-meeting intervention, which combined individual and group treatments, and in this manner, set up the possibility of utilizing ACT to treat individuals with chronic pain. This procedure was one of the main to address situation definition and clinical techniques handily with a chronic pain population. The subsequent protocol is an 8-meeting mediation that presents subjects common of a traditional CBT protocol (movement pacing, objective setting, schoolwork, etc.) There are also separate self-help books that give bit by bit guidelines. The self-improvement guides fill in as an introduction to the treatment as opposed to a protocol.

ACT applies 6 core treatment forms (ability to acknowledge, contact with the current second, watching oneself, cognitive defusion, values, and committed action) through various experiential activities to create psychological flexibility. The model is best represented by utilizing a hexaflex. An improved model may recommend that the intervention helps patients to turn out to be more open, present, and make a move.

Being Open

Patients figure out how to turn out to be more "open" to their experience of pain utilizing 2 standards: willingness to acknowledge (versus avoidance or escape) and cognitive defusion (versus combination with thoughts). The principle of willingness to acknowledge depicts the way toward allowing inside experiences (thoughts, emotions, body sensations, and memories) in regards to agony to go back and forth without struggling with or getting combined with them. When finding out about cognitive defusion, patients start to make good ways from thoughts, pictures, feelings, and memories and see them as what they seem to be. This can work to enable the patient to make good ways from these experiences and understand that they are not recognized by their opinions. Like this, the patient can work to react to these experiences through assessing their functionality given their qualities instead of accepting or "becoming tied up with" them in a literal way.

Being Present

Patients figure out how to turn out to be more "present" with their experience of pain utilizing 2 different principles: contact with the present moment (as opposed to living past or future) and watching oneself (versus dominance of the reasonable self). The standard of reaching the present moment describes how patients become more aware of and experience the present time and place. Care is fundamental to this procedure! Mindfulness is neither a special mystical state nor a type of relaxation and is an activity in simply seeing, or awareness. The purpose isn't to change or judge, but rather to be completely right now, seeing when the brain meanders and bringing it back. It includes having the option to work from a different and separated point of view.

The point of care is to build awareness of one's body capacities, feelings, and the content of thoughts. Every treatment meeting starts with a mindfulness exercise. Watching self involves patients getting to an excellent feeling of self, a congruity of consciousness that is always changing. Patients figure out how to contact their thoughts and emotions about pain from a separate observer.

Making a move

Patients also figure out how to "make a move" regardless of their experience of pain utilizing these ideologies: esteemed instructions (versus lack of standards clarity) and submitted activity (versus lack of steady activity). The guideline of valued directions describes the way toward finding what is generally imperative to one's actual self, regardless of whether it be self-awareness, recreation, citizenship, social connections, health, work/education, spirituality, family, child-rearing, as well as intimate relationships, child-rearing, as intimate relationships as well.

Making a committed activity includes the patient defining objectives as per their qualities and carrying them out responsibly. Patients have approached state and record commitments as explicit, measurable, achievable, realistic, and tangible steps that they are currently ready to take, alongside what exercises they are happy to do.

Toward the end of the intervention, patients are instructed how to keep up their progress by proceeding to:

- Practice mindfulness and acknowledgment works out

- Set short-term objectives every week

- Monitor their progress

Patients are also prepared for setbacks and relapse. When they have difficulty, as when they fail to live up or keep their responsibilities, they are prepared to commit once again to their action plan. At that point, the patient refocuses by seeing the setback and taking their awareness back to their valued directions. ACT has been appeared to have modest support, but CBT has strong, long-standing exploration to help the treatment of chronic, non-cancer pain, as per the American Psychological Association.

By what method can DBT Help Maintain Relationships

Most communication today is done digitally, using moment delegate, messaging, Snapchat, and so forth. In reality, as we know it where communication is readily available, it very well may be difficult to feel associated in a meaningful way.

Persuasive Behavior Therapy or DBT offers a whole module to teaching skills to help figure out how to communicate openly, more obviously, and in an expressive way. This component is called Interpersonal Effectiveness and concentrates on how you speak with others and provides skills to help uphold relations.

One of the ranges of abilities being instructed in the Interpersonal Effectiveness module is the G-I-V-E skill. This abbreviation shows relationship effectiveness. Relationship effectiveness speaks to the objective of a conflict-free or manageable conflict relationship. The G-I-V-E aptitude shows us the instruments expected to act. The other individual keeps on enjoying and respecting you, balancing immediate goals with the benefit of the long-term relationship, and keeping up relationship that issue to you.

G-I-V-E:

• Gentle — Being delicate methods being caring, non-judgmental, and respectful by the way we collaborate with someone else. Try to avoid accusing, shaming, or accusing someone else. Rather pose explaining questions if needed. Stay away from attacks, try to keep your voice "down," and be aware of your facials and non-verbal communication. If you approach others with respect, they are more likely to reciprocate.

• Interested — People love to be listened to. If you show interest in them, they will need to invest more energy with you. Regardless of whether you aren't generally that keen on the subject, show interest since you are keen on them. Look, gesture, ask follow-up questions, make an effort not to interrupt them, or change the subject. Surprisingly better than acting interested is being genuinely interested. I have found that there is continually something interesting if you focus, and others will see your efforts.

• Validate — Everyone needs to feel that their emotions are understood. If you approve somebody with your responses, you are showing you get them. You can do this with your terminologies, your arguments, just like your activities. Use intelligent tuning in to show you understand. Validation isn't equivalent to understanding; it tells somebody you regard their experience and offer the space to them.

• Easy Manner — Relax. Try to be receptive. Relax. Be happy and adaptable. In case you are trying with your emotions or state of mind, try to save them and focus on the other person. People appreciate spending time with people who are anything but difficult to be with. Not all things need to be a fight until the very end. This doesn't intend to abandon your values (yet that is a different DBT ability, F-A-S-T).

Effective Interpersonal abilities educated in DBT can improve the likelihood of positive outcomes in relationships and assist you in keeping up happy, healthy relationships for the long-term. When utilized effectively, G-I-V-E ability can empower you to have relationships based on a foundation of respect, integrity, empathy, and connection. If you remember this expertise, you ought to experience little difficulty keeping and maintaining relationships.

What are the troubles that people experience with connections?

Typically, after an initial period of "great relating regularly referred to as the honeymoon period," familiarity begins to set in, and tolerance levels may reduce. This may bring about increasing arguments and disagreements. However, these are not risky because two individuals with various foundations are most likely bound to have differences of opinion. The issue is the point at which the relationship can't figure out how to determine trouble so that there is a breakdown in communication and a little degree to improve.

Some valuable interpersonal abilities can assist you in managing social struggle, and these start from Dialectical Behavior Therapy or DBT, supported by the notion of dialectics. A dialectical perspective includes considering the two sides of a circumstance with the possibility that the world is formed of opposites. In a relational context, this may mean thinking that "love" and "hate" can both exist simultaneously, and like this, we figure out how to manage tension within interpersonal situations. The advantage of figuring out how to do this is an individual has a more decisional balance, which may prompt better choices. Here's a guide to show how dialectical thinking may be applied in a relational dilemma:

Partner A shows up home from work late as his train was delayed. He comes in to discover partner B, playing on his PlayStation. It is 8 pm, and A is hungry and a piece tired and irritable in the wake of the difficult day and the travel delay. He begins to feel angry that B has not put forth any attempt to prepare dinner as he is occupied in a game. In any case, an also really loves his partner and partakes in the time they spend together. Given this "love versus angry" position, partner A has some decision about how to act.

Does he...

Express outrage: moaning to B about his selfish behavior, which will presumably prompt a line and an unpleasant evening; or

Contain anger: avoiding a row and recommending they request a remove, so he gets food rapidly and ideally some pleasant time with his partner following a long and testing day?

Possibly you have encountered something similar, and maybe there were various manners by which you could have reacted to a partner, companion, youngster, or parent.

DBT offers practical direction in overseeing social difficulties to support healthy connections with others. Guiding can assist you in understanding how DBT abilities may enhance relationships throughout your life.

Helpful Tips for Improving Your Mental Focus

Keeping focused can be difficult, but it very well may be especially testing when you are surrounded by constant distraction. In the present consistently associated world, diversions are simply a click away.

In any event, during calm minutes, distraction is truly readily available as you wind up looking at your Instagram notifications or recent news updates.

The ability to focus on something in your condition and direct mental effort toward it is basic for learning new things, achieving objectives, and performing great over a wide variety of situations.

Regardless of whether you are trying to complete a report at work or contending in a marathon, your capacity to the center can mean the difference between success and failure.

Enlightening your intellectual focus is feasible, but that doesn't mean that it's quick and easy in any case. If it were simple, at that point, we would all have the extremely sharp concentration of a first-class competitor.

It will require some real effort on your part, and you may need to roll out certain improvements to a portion of your daily habits. Here are a few tips and tricks from psychology that can assist you in creating laser-like mental focus and concentration.

Survey Your Mental Focus

Before you begin working in the direction of improving your mental focus, you should start by surveying exactly how strong your mental focus is at the present moment.

In case the main set of statements appears to be more your style, at that point, you most likely as of now have fairly good concentration skills, but you could be significantly more grounded with a tiny exercise.

If you recognize more with the additional set of declarations, at that point, you likely need to work on your mental focus a lot, it may require some investment, but practicing some great habits and being aware of your distractibility can help.

Wipeout Distractions

While it might sound obvious, people frequently underestimate exactly what number of distractions keep them from focusing on the job needing to be done. Such intrusions may come as a radio blaring in the background or maybe an obnoxious co-worker who continually drops by your work area to talk.

Minimizing these sources of distraction isn't generally as simple as it sounds. While it may be as basic as turning off the TV or radio, you may think that it's substantially more challenging to manage an interrupting co-worker, spouse, child, or roommate.

One approach to manage this is to put aside a particular time and place and request to be disregarded for that timeframe. Another option is to search out a calm location where you realize you will have the option to work undisturbed. The library, a private room in your home, or even a quiet coffee shop, may all be acceptable spots to try.

A couple of procedures you should try to minimize or eliminate such internal interruptions are to ensure you are very much rested preceding the task and to utilize positive thoughts and imagery to fight off anxiety and worry. If you discover your mind wandering toward distracting thoughts, deliberately take your focus back to the job that needs to be done.

Limit Your Focus

While multitasking may be a great way to complete a lot done quickly, things being what they are, people are rather bad at it. Juggling multiple tasks without a moment's delay can dramatically cut down on productivity and make it a lot harder to focus on the significant details.

Think about your attention as a spotlight. If you shine that focus on one specific area, you can see things. In case you were trying to spread that equivalent measure of light over a large dark room, you may rather just impression the shadowy outlines.

Some portion of improving your psychological center is tied in with benefiting as much as possible from the resources you have available. Quit performing various tasks and rather focus on each thing in turn.

Live at the Time

It's hard to remain mental focus when you are ruminating about the past, stressing over the future, or listen to the current moment for some other clarification.

You have most likely heard people talk about the significance of "being present." It's everything about taking care of distractions, regardless of whether they are physical (your cell phone) or mental (your nerves) and being fully mentally engaged in the current moment.

This idea of being available is also basic for recovering your mental focus. Remaining engaged with the present time and place keeps your attention sharp, and your mental resources focused on the subtleties that truly matter at a particular point in time.

It might require some time but work on learning to live at the time genuinely. You can't change the past, and the future has not occurred at this point, but, what you do today can help you avoid repeating past mistakes and clear away for a more successful future.

Practice Mindfulness

Mindfulness is a current subject nowadays and in light of current circumstances. Despite the way that individuals have practiced types of care mindfulness meditation for thousands of years, its numerous medical advantages are as of late beginning to be understood.

In one study, researchers had HR experts take part in recreations of the kind of complex performing multiple tasks they occupied with every day at work.

These tasks must be finished in a short time and included answering phones, scheduling meetings, and writing notices with sources of data pouring in from various sources, including calls, emails, and text messages.

A portion of the members got two months of preparation in the utilization of mindfulness meditation. The outcomes found that only those who had gotten this preparation indicated improvement in concentration and focus.

Individuals from the meditation group had the option to remain focused longer, exchanged between tasks less now and again, and played out the work more productively than the other groups of participants.

Practicing mindfulness can include figuring out how to meditate, but it can also be as basic as trying a brisk and simple deep breathing exercise.

While this may appear to be a deceptively simple task, you may find that it is much more difficult than it shows up. Luckily, this breathing action is something you can do anyplace and whenever. In the long-term, you will perhaps find that it gets simpler to withdraw from invasive opinions and return your concentration to where it belongs.

Enjoy a Short Reprieve

Have you, at any point, tried to focus on something very similar for a long period? Sooner or later, your center begins to separate, and it turns out to be more and tougher to give your mental resources to the undertaking. That, however, your performance ultimately suffers as a result.

Traditional explanations in psychology have recommended this is because of attentional resources being depleted. Still, a few analysts accept that it has more to do with the brain's tendency to ignore sources of constant stimulation.

So whenever you are working on a prolonged task, such as setting up your taxes or reading for a test, make certain to offer yourself an occasional mental break.

Move your attention to something unrelated to the main job, regardless of whether it is just for a couple of seconds. These short moments of rest may mean that you can maintain your mental focus sharp and your success great when you truly need it.

Continue Practicing

Building your mental focus isn't something that will happen. Indeed, even professional athletes require a lot of time and practice to reinforce their fixation abilities.

One of the initial steps is to observe the effect that being diverted is having on your life. If you are trying to achieve your objectives and end up getting sidetracked by unimportant details, the time has come to begin putting a greater value on your time.

By creating your intellectual focus, you will find that you can achieve more and focus on the things in life that get you success, happiness, and satisfaction.

Chapter 14 - The Significance of Validation in Dialectical Behavior Therapy

Dialectical behavior therapy (DBT) associates cognitive and behavioral therapies with Eastern mindfulness practices. Created by therapist Marsha M. Linehan, DBT is valuable in rewarding people with a wide variety of issues, including misery, tension, bipolar, self-injury, dietary problems, substance misuse, and relationship struggle. The objective is for clients to figure out how to deal with their feelings and create healthier coping skills while also practicing self-acceptance.

The term dialectical refers to the objective of synthesizing the inflexible "black and white," considering numerous clients who experience difficulty controlling their feelings. Moreover, a key dialectical within DBT is the guideline of accepting the client as the person in question seems to be and offering validation, while also helping him/her learn change procedures. Validation in DBT refers to offering client verbal and non-verbal help and confirmation.

The emphasis on validation in DBT became out of observations in the late 1970s that numerous clients experienced social treatment as invalidating; this prompted resistance, and here and there withdrawal from treatment. Clients' resistance frequently showed in behaviors that sabotaged the viability of individual treatment. These observations prompted a portion of the core features of dialectical behavior therapy, including radical acknowledgment and approval of the client's current level of emotional and behavioral functioning. This adjusting of acknowledgment and change is significant within individual helpful communications yet within the general treatment. While the client learns abilities to develop self-acknowledgment, the specialist utilizes approval systems, including the following:

Techniques for Validation

1. Focus on listening with empathy and genuine concern, being mindful to remain at the time. Show interest through verbal and non-verbal signs: Nod and keep in touch, and utilize verbal answers, such as "Uh-huh" and "What else would you say you are feeling?"

2. Reply with the accurate likeness, summarizing what the individual had shared. For instance, "It seems like you are angry that your significant other made these plans without talking with you." Check for accuracy by asking, "Is that right?"

3. Observe and articulate the individual's unspoken emotions,

given what the person says and non-verbal cues. Ask if your observations are right. For instance, "Do you think it is unreasonable that she expects that you should appear on this occasion without asking you, is that right?"

4. Validate and restate the individual's feelings and behaviors corresponding to over significant time situations and issues. Recognize that their present feelings are understandable considering past experiences as well as present circumstances. For instance, "Taking into account that your mom was so controlling when you were growing up, it bodes well that you would feel resentment in this situation."

5. Focus on destructive behaviors that originate from earlier history, and point out why the present response isn't valuable. Repeat the previous experience and link it to the person's present issue and behavior choices. For instance, "Because your mom tried to control your time and exercises, it is understandable that you are feeling angry in this circumstance. However, refusing to speak your significant other doesn't assist her in understanding why you are so upset."

6. Focus on enabling the individual and regarding that person as an equivalent. While recognizing the client's struggles, express hope and optimism that the individual is fit for positive change. For instance, "I can see that you are buckling down on making changes, and I think you are going to see some improvement and begin feeling good."

In working with clients, DBT specialists are careful to abstain from negating practices and reactions than responses that dismiss, reject, or criticize the client's feelings and behaviors. Instances of this would include statements that the client ought not to "feel that way," that their assessment of the circumstance is inaccurate, that the issue isn't significant, or that the client is to be blamed for the problem.

Dr. Marsha Linehan, the maker of DBT, portrays six levels of validation, with each "level" offering a different tactic for approving somebody. As to interpersonal effectiveness, validation is valuable whether we look to better a relationship with a friend or family member, a friend, a colleague, or even somebody we've quite recently met. Approval is amazing to the point that it very well may be utilized to diffuse an antagonistic or escalating condition – since validating someone's point of view assists in reducing frustration and stress. How about we translate the six levels as to validating others.

1. Mindful commitment – Active attending is a good instance of this first degree of validation. Being available and showing interest non-verbally or potentially verbally, such as communicating your understanding by the method of gesturing, looking, and asking appropriate questions ("I hear you! What'd you do after she revealed to you that?")

2. Accurate reflection – Demonstrate to the individual you're tuning in to that their message is being received accurately. If

you decide to disagree, at any rate, the individual realizes that you are listening with intention, and that makes a difference ("I simply heard you state that your supervisor likes you, yet you don't believe you're doing a good job. Is it true that you are in effect unjustly hard on yourself?")

3. Reading signals – This includes some guesswork, and when you do this present, you should verbalize what you hear, with the goal that you can be corrected if you've misunderstood. You may think somebody is upset with you when they're essentially not feeling great, or the other way around. But, the way that you ask and help somebody share when they might be experiencing difficulty doing as such enhances the relationship ("You look troubled. Is something bothering you?")

4. Historical viewpoint – Drawing on your knowledge into somebody's prior experiences, you can loan point of view that helps the person come to an obvious conclusion about how they're feeling or how they're processing new information ("Possibly you don't confide in your new girlfriend because your past girlfriend cheated on you?")

5. Assuring reasonableness – Letting somebody realize that their thoughts, feelings, or behaviors are ordinary and very sensible. This gives reassurance, comfort, and sound point of view ("I see your frustration. A great many people would be annoyed at going through 30 minutes on hold with the link organization.")

6. Respectful honesty – Providing feedback that tells an individual that you regard them enough to "keep it genuine." This degree of approval is best conveyed with a backup of radical acknowledgment, alongside a non-judgmental position–considering that everybody has their strengths and limitations. Validating somebody with honesty and respect means regarding them as you'd need somebody to treat you in a private relationship ("I understand why you said that, yet I figure you could have had a better result if you utilized a softer tone?")

Despite which methods you use to validate somebody, the outcomes will undoubtedly be gainful. By the way, thank you for understanding this. We understand that you're busy, and we're thankful for your attention. Feels better, isn't that so?

Facilitating Partner Pain: Six Levels of Validation

If you have a friend or any member of your family with mental illness, compassion fatigue can set in rapidly. You, despite everything, love this individual. You are as yet dedicated to helping them show signs of improvement. And you also might be wondering, "Precisely when will we not need to manage this any longer?"

Nobody has the response to when mental illness will decrease or lessen by any means. We know the pain your loved one is experiencing–regardless of whether it is physical, mental, or both–is genuine. In any case, each individual has a subjective experience with comes to pain. For some people, they may work with a broken bone for quite a long time before realizing anything isn't right. For other people, a small paper cut is disturbing. Your job as a supportive loved one isn't to pass judgment on your partner's pain, but to acknowledge it is real, and to approve the experience.

A key point to understanding validation is to realize that "validation" doesn't also signify "understanding." Validation essentially means you are communicating to your cherished one, "I can hear you disclosing to me you are in torment, and it is alright to feel that way." Dr. Marsha Linehan, the maker of dialectical behavior therapy (DBT), identified six levels of validation. Each level increases in trouble, and if you just remain at a lower level with your loved one, it will, in any case accommodating. Dr. Linehan's work is focused on rewarding borderline personality disorder; however, her treatment has been demonstrated to work for a wide range of mental illnesses. Validation isn't only for those with mental illness, in any case: everybody has the right to realize they have been seen, heard, and adored, in any event, when they are in pain.

The first level of validation is available. When was the last time you focused on your loved one? Numerous individuals are uncomfortable with the feelings of others since they either don't have any idea how to react or find their own uncomfortable emotions rising to the surface. Being available when the exceptional feeling is expressed isn't simple, but worth the effort as an approach to help your loved one.

The second level of validation is the exact reflection. When you are reflecting the thoughts and feelings of your loved one, you verbalize what you have heard. Precise reflection can seem like, "In this way, I hear you saying you are frustrated that your energy level is low," or "I can enlighten you are feeling restless concerning heading off to the gathering today around evening time." The key is not to be a parrot, repeating your loved one's words verbatim, as that can seem as though you are sarcastic instead of being supportive.

The third level of validation is reading an individual's behavior and think about what they may be feeling. Numerous individuals are withdrawn from their emotions. There are numerous reasons behind this, including having an invalidating environment as a child, where they were told they did not have the feeling they were experiencing ("No, you are not hungry - you just ate!" or "Pleasant young ladies don't blow up" or "Young men don't cry.") Your loved one may also confuse emotions, such as thinking excitement is anxiety or anger is sadness. Or then again, your loved one may have discovered that others don't respond well when they show their feelings, so they keep locked down tightly. In this level of validation, you may state something like, "I'm guessing that remark from your supervisor was harmful."

Your loved one may correct you, and that is alright. It was only a supposition, and your loved one is the expert on his/her feelings.

The fourth level of validation is understanding the person's behavior as far as their history and biology. We respond to the world dependent on our previous experiences and biological wiring. If we have had a negative experience, future situations like past experiences may cause a bad reaction. For instance, if your loved one was bitten and scratched by a feline as a youngster, s/he might not have any desire to associate with cats now. A case of how you can approve this may be, "Given your experiences with felines, I understand why you would not have any desire to head off to someplace where there are three cats in the house."

The fifth level of validation is normalizing or recognizing emotional reactions that anybody would have. Realizing that others would probably feel the equivalent in a similar situation assists in decreasing the negative emotions, your loved one might be having. This may seem like, "obviously, you are anxious about the prospective employee meeting - everybody feels anxious when doing something this significant," (however, don't line this up with, "You will be fine," which negates the previous statement of validation).

The 6th level of validation is radical genuineness. What is "radical genuineness"? It regards your loved one as a real individual with real emotions rather than as somebody who has a mental illness and is incapable of understanding his/her issues. When you express radical genuineness, you are meeting your loved one as an equal, and communicating both your help just as your belief that s/he can solve his/her issues.

DBT Decoded: Willingness vs. Obstinacy

While looking at the DBT idea of Willingness versus Willfulness, we perceive how Dialectical Behavior Therapy indeed presents us with a pair of opposite forces at play within the mind. Remember that the focal idea of dialectical thinking is that we frequently hold contradicting perspectives simultaneously—and the nearness of these thoughts holds the potential for conflict. The way to well-being is to recognize their quality and the potential for struggle—but to decide to "dance, not wrestle" with them. All in all, would you say you are willing or obstinate? Eagerness is our capacity to take the path of least resistance—to rehearse radical acknowledgment with our circumstance and what life hands us—and to be a functioning member. Ask any behavioral health professional, and they'll mention to you what a delight it is to work with a client who is willing. In fact, as a rule, the first goal of treatment is to assist somebody in seeing that there's an expectation, because without trust, why try? For what reason would anybody do something if the outcome is sure to be a failure? The reason to be willing is that we don't have any idea what's in store; however, we do realize that achievement is just success is only available for those who try.

The universe rewards ability! Willfulness is the opposite. Acting willfully is attempting to twist the universe to your wants and needs, paying little heed to what's possible. In dynamic substance misuse, the individual may practice willfulness by proceeding to act irresponsibly and waiting that the world will change to address their issues. Being willful is to look down on radical acceptance–taking a place that you need not acknowledge what is–and figuring you can will your way through a universe that rotates around you. Performing deliberately is something that we've all done sooner or later in our life. Small kids act willfully when they defy their parents' instructions and do essentially what they need to do–right or wrong. Child-rearing can be incredibly baffling when one fights to discover that there are times when you can't change the will of a child; you can just change your strategy for communication. When you ask somebody effective in their recovery from liquor or potential drug use about how they did it, you'll frequently hear a reaction like, "I was prepared."

When you're prepared, you're receiving a place of readiness. When you're not, that is your stubborn willfulness saying, "I'll keep on acting irresponsibly, and it will end up being alright regardless." The willing individual is a liberal member of life. The willful person is unreasonable and decides to remain uninvolved. As we consider the attitude of willingness versus willfulness, we can perceive the number of good open doors for the individuals who are willing and what number of chances are missed by the individuals who act willfully.

What would we be able to do to cultivate willingness, when our temperament toward something causes us to feel willful? We can observe the golden rule—to change something, and we should first recognize it. Next time you feel stuck, ask yourself, "Am I acting willfully? Am I deciding to ignore the facts and remaining attached to what I need?" Once we watch such an attitude, we can settle on the conscious choice to get unstuck, do what we naturally know to be a wiser choice—and let it all out! Some of the time, it's a matter of taking a chance, accepting that life is loaded up with the unknown, and that life requires risk in exchange for a reward. For certain individuals, the idea that gets them unstuck is becoming comfortable with discomfort (and doing it at any rate). Others motivate themselves by truly making a move that lines up with willingness, with the understanding that where the body drives, the brain will follow. Whatever it takes, pick ability, and appreciate being a functioning member in this great experience known as life.

The sympathetic and highly trained, Futures Recovery Healthcare group endeavors to give instruction, support, and behavioral treatments related to drugs at the best possible occasions to promote a successful recovery from a substance abuse disorder. Call today to find out about our particular and effective treatment programs.

DBT Decoded: Walking the Middle Path

"You overstate more than anybody in the entire world!" If you have ever partaken in a difference that escalated into extreme statements, such as this one, at that point, you realize that it is so difficult to go to an understanding once either or the two gatherings become captivated in their reasoning. One similitude that assists in explaining dialectical thinking, the establishment for DBT (Dialectical Behavioral Therapy), is walking the Middle Path. If you leave DBT with one careful device for significantly upgrading close relationships, this is in the same class

"To Walk the Middle Path" implies replacing "either-or" thinking with community-oriented "both-and" thinking. Again and again, we cause up our brains about how we feel about something utilizing a high contrast, win big or bust, dynamic development. When we do this, we run the risk of being to leave balance—not giving deserved validation to another perspective. When we can't help contradicting somebody, it might be normal to accept that they are wrong, and we are correct. Yet, is this necessarily how it is? Not if we adopt a dialectical approach to our thinking, appreciating that there's in every case more than one approach to see something. When we replace, "it is possible that I'm correct or they are right," with "I'm correct and they are right," at that point, we can consider each to be as a feeling as opposed to absolute truth.

When we walk the Middle Path, we prepare for a bargain. When that compromise validates our feelings and those of another, we are on the way to a more harmonious outcome. Think about the consequences of extreme thinking. Frequently, it prompts extreme feelings—either excessively sincerely contributed or "looking at" totally, because of frustration. Once in a while, extraordinary reasoning makes us too rigid or too loose. We make an over the top circumstance or excessively little of it.

On the other hand, acknowledgment and change are most available when we decide to walk the Middle Path. In doing such, we become unstuck. We gain flexibility, with the goal that we can esteem our point of view in proper balance to the opinions of others. Strolling the Middle Path makes the sort of liberality that facilitates fairness and respect. Simply, it's an incredible mentality for making peace and contentment.

The humane and highly trained, Futures Recovery Healthcare

group endeavors to give training, support, and behavioral therapies related to drugs at the correct occasions to advance a successful recovery from a substance abuse disorder. Call today to find out about our particular and powerful treatment programs.

The "Savvy Mind" ACCEPTS

A lot of Dialectical Behavioral Therapy's effectiveness for motor control and relapse prevention can be attributed to the memory helpers utilized in its teachings. Some DBT ideas give rich visual associations, such as walking the Middle Path and Turning the Mind. Others, such as ACCEPTS, utilize abbreviations that are anything but difficult to review and help aggregate a lot of strategies for achieving a shared objective. On account of ACCEPTS, a DBT trouble resistance range of abilities, the prompt objective is to occupy the psyche sufficiently long to intercede in an emotional reaction to an upsetting circumstance. Like all aptitudes, the more we practice, the more productive we become with our capacity to call upon it when required. Along these lines, we should do a little DBT decoding and explore how our Wise Mind ACCEPTS.

A – Activities. Once in a while, the best way to deal with offer the brain a break from stress-inducing stimuli is to get physically busy. Here, we can call upon interests, tasks, or different exercises that serve to pick up consideration. Playing guitar, taking a stroll, arranging a storeroom, food shopping, or playing Frisbee are, for the most part, good examples. If you decide to achieve a chore, at that point, you're taking out two targets with one shot—you're effectively distracting yourself and finishing a necessary task at the same time.

C – Contributing. Regardless of whether you decide to chip in an ideal opportunity for a network cause, help a friend who's shorthanded at work, or on the other hand, keep an eye on the nephew, you're doing something productive that requires focus. Adding to the needs of another person can assist us in feeling great about ourselves as well, and building confidence is consistently something worth being thankful for. In the interim, we're achieving the objective of distraction, allowing us to quiet down and settle on a greater choice.

C – Comparisons. As people, we can't resist the urge to compare ourselves with others. The purpose of this distraction technique is to increase point of view by making such comparisons. Some of the time, we should simply look at our circumstance now versus a past time when we were considerably worse off to recover a sense of gratitude. It might be enlightening to consider people who live in impoverished conditions, or the individuals who have limited access to companions and friends and loved ones, to remember exactly how blessed we are compared with those who have less.

E – Opposite Emotions. Such is the idea of DBT that we as often as possible use opposites to assist us in returning to, or keep up the middle ground. For instance, we can tune in to music that satisfies us to counterbalance feelings of sadness. Anger might be reduced by viewing a comedy routine that never fails to produce giddiness. Anxiousness might be alleviated by discovering quiet in the act of meditation or essentially reading a spiritual book.

P – Pushing Away. While the previously mentioned procedures give us a perception of making a beeline for something, driving away is tied to keeping up our ground and sending upsetting ideas away. Since our brain might need to hold on to stress, accepting that we need it, we may utilize strategies that help us compartmentalize our thoughts, even if we place them aside to be addressed later. We also may assume complete responsibility for these thoughts, record them on a bit of paper, and consume it. In doing as such, we demonstrate our capacity to drive away what doesn't serve us, maybe banishing such thoughts for all time (if not, there's in every case more paper and matches!)

T – Thoughts. Diverting with thoughts is a bag of tricks that we save close by for crisis use. These are our "go-to" thoughts that essentially and quickly distract our mind–giving important opportunity to process whatever is causing newfound stress. This may incorporate checking to ten or reciting the Serenity

Prayer.

S – Sensations. Now and again, stress overcomes us so rapidly that we have to approach a time tested physical sensation to wake us up and give flashing interruption. Cold water sprinkled on the face may do it. For a few, it's the quieting sound of a chime or a hard rock melody that gets the heart racing. It worth trying different things with a physical impression that is anything but difficult to call upon and goes about as a trigger to take you back to your faculties—and remind you not to exude the little stuff (and that it's everything, little stuff).

As should be obvious, this DBT abbreviation is effective for helping us remember this significant arrangement of distraction procedures. The DBT skills we practice empower us to more readily tolerate pressure, act carefully, and control our feelings. In doing as such, we stay in charge, use sound judgment, and keep up healthy interpersonal relationships that we are so blessed to have a Wise Mind!

The empathetic and highly trained, Futures Recovery Healthcare group strives to give training, support, and behavioral treatments related to meds at best possible occasions to advance an effective recovery from a substance abuse disorder. Call today to find out about our particular and successful treatment programs.

DBT Decoded: Mindfulness "How Skills" in real life

The How Skills: Non-Judgmentally, One-Mindfully, and effectively are exercises that add to healthy mindfulness practice.

Non-Judgmentally – The demonstration of taking a non-critical position. To start observing our thoughts and emotions equitably, we should focus on being non-judgmental about them. Inside our careful practice, there is nothing but bad thoughts, unwanted thoughts, or welcomed thoughts. They are on the whole equivalent since we don't pass judgment. Some portion of the help we involvement with care is letting go of our opinions. By doing so, we're ready to let go of the stress that originates from trying to oppose what causes us torment. Such resistance can turn into a contributing element, or even the source, of suffering. Since we're human and judgment is inside our nature, we're probably going to be tested by this piece of mindful practice. That is alright. When we notice ourselves judging, we realize that we've wandered from care, and we start once more. Care is a get-away from judgment, so we don't pass judgment on ourselves for resistance. We notice, treat ourselves with comprehension and empathy—and start once more. Like the ballplayer who tries to make a shot, the non-judgmental approach of care is much the same as the great procedure of having a fair position. With legs shoulder-width, and the body facing the crate, we set up for a successful shot.

One-Mindfully – The demonstration of focusing on each thing in turn. This is something contrary to performing various tasks, a typical habit related to our modern, overstimulated environment. By taking part in undertakings with one-mindfulness, we strengthen our capacity to participate in each training in turn. Reflection is a one-mindfully practice that allows us to center our brain and let go of distractions. Inside our regular day-to-day existence, we can act one-carefully by basically finishing an errand without delaying to check email, pick up the telephone, or worry about another pending undertaking. We can decide to cook, eat, play music, tune in, swim, or do anything one-mindfully. With our brain focused on the basket—thinking just about the strength and projection expected to finish the shot—One-Mindfulness gives us the best chance for flawless execution.

Viably – The act of applying mindful concepts, learning, and sharpening our training. To be viable implies that we advance and reinforce our careful muscles as we move along. As we practice care, we become more mindful of the spaces between our thoughts and our actions–giving ourselves a freshly discovered capacity to decrease impulsivity–a particularly important device for people recovering from the sickness of fixation. Becoming more skillful at the act of care improves our capacity to effectively reduce judgment (of ourselves as well as other people), let go of feelings that block us, and nurture our feeling of sympathy. The act of starting again when we notice our brain wandering is effective to act that strengthens our resilience. Just expressed, when we practice mindfulness effectively, the positive takeaways are unlimited. With a non-judgmental position framing the base of sound procedure and our ability to center one-carefully, all that is left is to make an effort effectively. Hit or miss, it's a wondrous thing.

Care in addiction treatment

Care based pressure the management strategies have been demonstrated successful in the treatment of stress and anxiety-based disorders. When fused into a balanced psychological health or addiction treatment program, the act of mindfulness through mindfulness-based stress reduction (MSBR) can give patients a helpful instrument to control the impacts of nervousness, fear, alarm, and different pressure related emotional wellness issues.

How do I practice mindfulness?

"Care" is another method of saying "seeing the little things at the time." Actively being in your current second can assist you in avoiding obsessing on the past, worrying about the future, or in any case, drowning in emotional responses to upsetting issues. To a few, it might be quite difficult. Closing off the psyche can be difficult. So how would you do it? There are different techniques. Focusing on your breath and breathing is a great spot to begin. Focusing on only the breath traveling every which way from the body, feeling it enter the nose, fill the lungs, and leave the body can be a positive starting practice in care. During this period, there should be no dynamic ideas in your mind. You are to never really see your breath. Another approach to describe the training is to characterize it as a type of meditation in which you quiet your internal discourse and spotlight exclusively on the vibes.

What illnesses advantage from the use of mindfulness?

Any emotional well-being issue described by a sleeping disorder, a decreased capacity to manage stress, increased anxiety, or depression would profit by a treatment plan that incorporates mindfulness for stress management. This incorporates:

- Eating issue. Mindfulness, acknowledgment, and self-analysis all decrease for individuals struggling with bulimia, anorexia, or eating disorders after MSBR treatment.

- Anxiety issue. Summed up tension issue has been appeared to improve with care treatment.

- Panic attacks. Fits of anxiety can be moderated when MSBR methods are utilized.

- Phobias. The mind-boggling nature of fears can be decreased when care is worked on during the pressure time frame.

- Depression. Improved temperament has been related to MSBR methods too.

- Substance abuse. Various issues identified with substance recovery—sleep deprivation, passionate upheavals, sorrow, nervousness, and so on—can be improved by the act of care.

How fast does the exercise of mindfulness produce results?

The quiet and quieting impacts of care and thought increment after some time. The more you practice, the more lasting the positive effects throughout your life, and the more rapidly you will start to see a reduction of the effect of pressure.

Is mindfulness about sitting still?

Regardless of the way that the goal is to even now the brain, it isn't important to, in any case, the body. Numerous individuals find that the best profit by care procedures learned in pressure on the board when they plan something to possess their hands. Concentrating on the breath while rehearsing a detached action can build the quieting impacts and decrease the odds that your inner dialogue will drown out your peace. While practicing care, a few people appreciate:

- Gardening

- Walking or running

- Knitting

- Cleaning the house

- Listening to soft music (as a rule without lyrics) or playing music

Is mindfulness-based stress reduction right for you?

Nearly everybody can profit by incorporating the strategies and methods of reasoning of mindfulness into their lives. Yet, most who are struggling with issues like an eating disorder or substance abuse will quite often find that their involvement with treatment improves when they practice mindfulness. If you might want more data, get in touch with us at Futures today.

Reclaim Your Life with These 5 Steps to Restoring Balance

You open your telephone, and instantly, you're bombarded by warnings.

There's another phone message, missed calls, comments on your Facebook, your life partner mentioning you stop for something in the way home, writings from collaborators requesting that you go out, and at least a dozen unread emails.

And that is exactly what's going on with your telephone.

It appears there will never be sufficient time in the day to stay aware of your hectic way of life. Your to-do list is for all time growing and never complete.

Luckily, you needn't bother with a genie to give you the desire of additional time or an army of clones to make your offering.

The truth is that you can find a healthy lifestyle. You can avoid being overpowered. You can avoid wearing out. You can complete everything and still put resources into life's significant stuff.

Here are a couple of steps to assist you in upgrading your time, assume back responsibility for your life, and make the balance you so desperately need.

Learn to say no

In the world of steady and ever-increasing connections, there's an endless array of exercises to do each moment of the day. We're present during a time of suffering from FOMO (fear of missing out) since we're shackled by our limited measure of time to take an interest in these happenings.

But, in case you're looking for a more focused self, it's an ideal opportunity to figure out how to say no. Say no a great deal! Disapprove of everything except those things that are helping you arrive at your objectives or make you happier.

From the start, it might be hard to turn down loved ones, yet by and large, by helping yourself conserve your energy, you will be more available to them for the occasions that truly matter.

Activity Step: Turn down a plan that doesn't energize you and invest that energy rather reviving and relaxing at home.

Minimize

The minimalist and tiny home developments aren't only a few hippies attempting to live out of leads. It's a community built on an establishment of focusing on what's extremely significant throughout everyday life.

Conclusion

I hope you enjoyed the journey and in this book, we have discovered that in view of the consequences of this examination, DBT skills can altogether diminish the seriousness of insanity and patients' depressed mind-set, however, had a slight and non-significant impact in improving depression, emotional control, anger, nervousness, positive warmth, and executive performance.